*Discovering the Four Facets of a Godly Woman*

# Woman OF Splendor

*Discovering the Four Facets of a Godly Woman*

## LINDA WEBER

BROADMAN
& HOLMAN
PUBLISHERS

Nashville, Tennessee

0-8054-1844-X

Published by Broadman & Holman Publishers, Nashville, Tennessee
Editorial Team: Vicki Crumpton, Janis Whipple, Kim Overcash
Typesetting and Design: PerfecType, Nashville, Tennessee

Dewey Decimal Classification: 248.8
Subject Heading: WOMEN—RELIGIOUS LIFE / WOMEN—
CONDUCT OF LIFE
Library of Congress Card Catalog Number: 99-30455

Chapter 7 is revised from a previously published chapter by Linda Weber,
contributing author to *The Joy of a Promise Kept* (Sisters, Ore.: Multnomah, 1996).
Used by permission.
The Four Pillars of Manhood chart is from *Tender Warrior,* by Stu Weber
(Sisters, Ore.: Multnomah, 1993). Used by permission.

Unless otherwise stated all Scripture citation is from the NASB, the New
American Standard Bible, © the Lockman Foundation, 1960, 1962, 1963, 1968,
1971, 1972, 1973, 1975, 1977; used by permission. Also cited are The Holy Bible,
King James Version; The Holy Bible, New International Version (NIV),
copyright © 1973, 1978, 1984 International Bible Society; and AMP, the Amplified
Bible, Old Testament © 1962, 1964 by Zondervan Publishing House, used by
permission, and the New Testament © The Lockman Foundation
1954, 1958, 1987, used by permission.

Library of Congress Cataloging-in-Publication Data
Weber, Linda, 1947–
    Woman of splendor : discovering the four facets of a godly woman / Linda
    Weber.
        p.  cm.
    Includes bibliographical references.
    ISBN 0-8054-1844-X (hardcover)
    1. Women—Religious life.   2. Women—Conduct of life.   3. Christian life.
4. Woman (Theology)
    I. Title.
    BV4527.W4          1999
    248.8'43—dc21

                                                                    99-30455
                                                                       CIP

1 2 3 4 5  03 02 01 00 99

# *Dedication*

To my three wonderful daughters (in-law) —
Carolyn, Jami Lyn, and Jessica.


What feminine pleasure each of you has brought into my life!


The last version of my *Apron Strings* has now been given.
I thank God for bringing you into my boys' lives,
and into Dad's and mine as well.

## Apron Strings #3
### For Carolyn

For many years at tuck-in time
we've prayed for our dear Kent
That God would shine His light through him
fulfilling this tall twig's bent.

We also prayed most earnestly
from the time he was a baby,
For just that perfect wife for Kent
to be groomed and saved to be his lady.

Off to Oxford he did go
Among so many ventures;
Little did he know he'd find
the one for lifelong pleasures.

That one and only Carolyn Drake
said yes to his big question,
Our firstborn son, our last to wed,
brings changes to the equation.

Loyalty to you, his Princess Dear,
supercedes his mama now;
The tears may come as I adjust
to this godly, serious vow.

And so I give you apron strings
from winding 'round my heart;
Entwined around my little boy,
and now they're cut apart.

Although Kent's gone for ten years now
from our home where he grew up,
It is still a must I cut this cord,
As it's with you he now comes to sup.

We'll always love our Rooskie boy,
this fine young man so bright;
It's been sheer joy to train this man,
Now give him to you this night.

I'm not sure you can know the real joy I do feel
as I receive you as my daughter;
Oxford or no, I write you this poem,
that my heart is made known as a starter.

In regard to these strings that I do cut away,
the truth is that I *now* get you both,
To view as one flesh and honor as one
because of this incredible oath.

Most likely our God will bring children to you;
Dad jokes as he thinks of your height.
There may be some basketball stars up ahead
as those days are just out of our sight.

That Weber generation, yet to become,
is the heritage we're thanking God for;
He's answering our prayers as He sheds us
much grace,
to fulfill His dear plan with splendor.

Carolyn, dear, we accept you just now
into our family with much pride;
May we all do our best to seek God faithfully
in His presence forever abide.

I love you, Carolyn,
Mom Weber

Written by Linda Weber and presented to her newest daughter-in-law, Carolyn, the night of Kent and Carolyn's wedding rehearsal dinner, October 11, 1997.

# Table of Contents

*Acknowledgments*                                                    ix

*Introduction*                                                        1

*Part One:*   BASIC CONSIDERATIONS
Chapter 1    Confusing Images                                        4
Chapter 2    Biblical Authority                                     14
Chapter 3    Differences between Masculine and Feminine             21
Chapter 4    The Jewel of Femininity                                35

*Part Two:*   Facet #1 - HELPMATE MEANT TO PARTNER
Chapter 5    A Helpmate Suitable                                    44
Chapter 6    Commitment, Submission, and Rebellion                  61
Chapter 7    Building Your Marriage                                 83

*Part Three:* Facet #2 - NURTURER MEANT TO DEVELOP
Chapter 8    The Nurturing Process                                  98
Chapter 9    Feeling Nurtured or Not                               119
Chapter 10   Letting Go—the Culmination                            144

*Part Four:* Facet #3 - RELATER MEANT TO CONNECT
Chapter 11     The Relational Genius                        160
Chapter 12     Importance of Being a Hub                    170
Chapter 13     Connecting Past to Present and Future        180

*Part Five:* Facet #4 - DESIGNER MEANT TO BEAUTIFY
Chapter 14     The Wonderful Female Body                    192
Chapter 15     Transforming Fragments into Beauty           201
Chapter 16     Expression Made through Details              209

*Conclusion*                                                217

*Appendix A:* Feeling Nurtured or Not—                      220
*Appendix B:* Being a Hub in the Home                       223
*Appendix C:* Being a Hub with Children                     226
*Appendix D:* Being a Hub in an Office/Business/Life Setting  229

*Study Questions*                                           231

*Endnotes*                                                  238

*Charts and Illustrations*
Pillars Chart                                               33
The Jewel of Femininity                                     34
A Helpmate Suitable                                         60
Biblical Submission                                         82
Process Required for Product                                103
Am I Nurturing My Child Beyond the Obvious Physical Realm?  106
The Impact of a Nurturing Mom's Process                     118
Nurtured or Not?                                            124

# Acknowledgments

*I* am full of appreciation for the large team of players who have come around me for this intense season to spur me on and see this book "get off the ground." Having come through a building project not long ago, I see that writing a book is a lot like building a house. It takes a long time to plan, to choose the key factors to incorporate, and to find the skillful team who will faithfully stick with you till the end and make sure you are coordinating the many pieces at the right time and in the right order. The finished product is heavily affected by those who participate. I'm looking forward to moving in soon, having finalized things with the title company.

I thank my husband, Stu, for his encouragement and excitement for me. He affirms me as he sacrifices his agenda to allow my getting this message out to help women feel validated in their femininity. I thank him for the privilege of sharing together in giving out God's message to men and women. This "Tender Warrior" is my hero.

My adult "kids" have all been so supportive, making special trips to gather for book planning, editing, locating quotes, and choosing a title. Their calls to check up on me and to remind me of their prayers have been affirming. Thanks to Kent and Carolyn, Blake and Jami Lyn, and Ryan and Jessica for upholding me. An extra measure of gratitude goes to Blake for all his work as my agent.

There has been power in the prayers. I've felt the impact, and I thank my fervent prayer team for their diligent work, which is the backbone of any victory. The following diligent women sent reassuring notes of remembrance and called regularly for updates, asking how to pray: June Lininger (my mom), Shirley Embanks, Jan Nowowieski, Beth Schaeffer, Paula Shelden, and Carolyn Thomas. Many others participated in the extended prayer team as well.

The typing/computer team was a major piece in this puzzle. Besides praying for me and encouraging me, Pam Leone got the first half of the project off the ground. Nora Schriener with her husband, Chuck, helped me along for the next season. Then Joan Petersen made a lot happen toward the end with her incredible expertise. You did so much more than the basics, Joan. Wow! All were essential in this major project, as I tried to learn about computer translations and numerous technical intricacies. Thanks from the bottom of my heart. I couldn't have done it without each of you. Also thanks to Barry Arnold, Steve Overby, and Donna Stern for the computer consultations.

I am deeply grateful for each of you who were manuscript readers. Your prayers, food treats, errands, and love for this project will not be forgotten. Thanks so much to this great group: Carolyn Weber, Linda Campbell, Christy Canzler, Myrna Alexander, Anita Bailey, Judy Tygert, Cyndi Strandberg, Donna Harris, Judy Taylor, Annie Darby, Becky Nelson, Eva Turnbull, Vicki Leenders, and Dorothy and Byron Weber. Our extended times of working together have been most helpful. Thanks to Pam, Nora, and Joan for all the reading and editing help as well as your computer work.

To Donna Campbell, I thank you for the terrific home you made available on the Oregon coast to get so much done in solitude. What an opportunity for inspiration!

To Sandy Wilson, I thank you for the privilege of working to clarify together so many women's issues. The fruit of it all can be passed down to many others—thanks, friend.

Interviews with many have been appreciated. Thanks especially to Annie, Connie, and Betty who each gave me lengthy consultations.

Mike Petersen, your encouragement for me and this venture is remembered and appreciated. Thank you.

Thanks to Deb Strubel for your long-distance editing work. Your careful attention to detail was very helpful in making things come together well.

To my Broadman & Holman team, I am very grateful to be in partnership with you. Thanks for believing in this project and in me. Vicki Crumpton, you have been lots of fun and skillful in your work. Thanks for all you are and do. Janis Whipple, for all your work and careful attention, I thank you for your extra-mile attitude. Kim Overcash, I thank you for your ongoing labors of love to put so many editorial pieces together as well. For helping women through choosing to publish and distribute this book, we all thank you.

# Introduction

My husband and I have a multitalented friend, Steve Tucker, who crafts intricately detailed pencil drawings. As he studied an old Indian likeness he was about to give my husband, he knew something wasn't quite right. He could not put his finger on what needed changing. Finally, it occurred to him that placing the drawing in front of a mirror would present a new angle from which to consider the dilemma. "Yes, of course!" he shouted. "I see the problem." It took a different point of view to capture the elusive secret of setting right the entire picture.

In our feminine journey, a new perspective can enable us to pursue avenues we need to explore. I feel called to share with you the keys I have gathered over the years that can open some gates. I hope it will be like taking the inspiring scenic route instead of the interstate. May God help me do this to His honor.

Ecclesiastes 1:9 reminds us that "there is nothing new under the sun." But sometimes looking at the same old truths from a different angle sparks our understanding. It is my desire that this presentation of femininity would thrust you into new levels of pleasure and fulfillment.

Maybe you are one of those many women who is searching for a missing ingredient. You've pursued various options to no avail. Although frustrated, you continue to search because you not only want but also desperately need some answers. Culturally, you have been bombarded with worldly "solutions" which only prove to be transient, hollow, and false. You may have even heard plenty of Bible verses tossed about. Even in the face of truth, the pieces seem disjointed, and the overall vision fragmented. Tapping back into biblical teachings with a revived perspective can revolutionize your life. As you adjust your outlook, you will most likely experience a dawning so bright that you'll exclaim, like Steve, "Yes, of course! I see the problem."

"Thy word is a lamp to my feet, / And a light to my path" (Psalm 119:105). God *is* our illumination source. By understanding the "God factor" in putting the pieces of our feminine vision together, we will see more clearly practical applications of age-old biblical truths for the present-day woman.

# PART 1

# *Basic Considerations*

# *Confusing Images*

*A* young girl came home from school and announced to her mom that she had learned how to prevent AIDS.

*Oh my!* her mom thought, disappointed at not having been the first one to inform her daughter of this sexually related issue.

The girl proceeded to tell her mom the magic formula: "All you have to do is buy condominiums and avoid intersections."

Well, we should expect some confusion at this young level. Yet there is plenty of confusion remaining at the adult level about even the basics of sexual identity.

If you have heard about how glorious it is to be a woman, maybe you haven't experienced the splendor. Women today don hard hats, descend on formerly all-male military academies, or complain about the corporate glass ceiling. Other women quit jobs to stay home full-time with children,

4

yet struggle to feel appreciated for the clean laundry and hot meals they produce.

If you have never seen godly femininity modeled, it's hard to relate. You may feel like the little girl who lived in a very cloudy part of the country. She had never seen the blue sky. She had heard it was up there, but until she got in an airplane and flew above the clouds, she never had opportunity to see it in all its splendor.

"Wow!" she said. "This is beautiful."

Being a feminine woman of splendor means we reflect the glory of God through four specific facets that will be discussed in this book. God designed woman to be a helper, a nurturer, a relater, and a designer. By examining and understanding these four facets, we will develop a balanced view of femininity.

# Half-Truths

In a court of law, a witness is asked, "Do you swear [on this Bible] to tell the truth, the whole truth, and nothing but the truth, so help you God?" The judge is not asking for half of the story or a half-truth.

People who use half-truths from Scripture (or elsewhere) are distorting the truth, which is the same as lying. It is imperative that we examine God's intentions. Otherwise, when it comes to understanding basic truths like femininity and masculinity, we come up short. God designed two genders with their own special traits to reflect His full image.

The devil deludes us with incredible sophistication. He doesn't approach us with cloven hooves, horns, and a pitchfork. He comes disguised as an angel of light. Genesis 3:1 tells us he was "more crafty than any beast of the field." Satan takes a partial truth and exaggerates it until it becomes a vice.

For example, there is nothing wrong with wanting to be fulfilled; but when that desire is taken to extremes and self-fulfillment is put above the good of others, it becomes a vice. Some in our culture are deceived into thinking that self-orientation (selfishness/narcissism) produces genuine fulfillment. "I," "me," and "my" are central to their world.

When a woman sees herself as central to all—more important or better than she is—she often feels compelled to demonstrate to herself and others that she is as superior as she wishes to be. This concentration on self distracts from her ability to adapt by giving of herself as a marriage partner, a nurturer, a relater, or a designer. Selfishness stifles the feminine expression. Confusion prevails since she has "bought" a half-truth of femininity.

# Following the Current

One young lady had been very attractive and "feminine," if you will. She was the first young woman in her class to fall in love with her "prince charming" and get married. She appeared to be living in the "usual" feminine way. Then, little by little, her underlying disenchantment surfaced. She clipped her graceful curls. She eliminated make-up. She wore men's clothing. Wanting complete freedom to express herself, she left her husband of many years.

Many women are searching for meaning; they want to know who they are and what they are meant to be. But where are they looking? Culture tells women to fulfill themselves. It's so easy to allow the pull of culture's current to drown us in gender death and to resurrect us in unisex. Our culture prides itself in its diversity and yet is out to destroy the most obvious form: the God-created differences of men and women. The blurring of sexual distinctions has caused much confusion, which is blasphemy to the full image of God.

# Too Close to Home

The power of the current remains etched in my mind from a vacation experience in southern California. I was enjoying the sun on a sandy beach with my friend, along with thousands of others. Suddenly, a lifeguard some distance behind us urgently dashed through the crowd toward an emergency he had spotted. Kathy and I remarked that he must see something important, which we couldn't spot. As he entered the water, he jumped into his flippers to expedite his swim. Curious, we followed his path with our eyes.

Then we saw it. A swimmer was in trouble. A hush fell over the crowd.

To my amazement, the person in danger was one of my sons. He was close to other family members and yet none of us had seen the danger signs this alert lifeguard recognized. Wow! The deadly currents could have carried my boy under if the lifeguard had not taken action. I'm grateful to a young man I was never able to thank.

Are we focused on the current swirling around us? We must be as vigilant as that lifeguard. If our femininity is in any kind of danger, we must rush to protect the beauty of our womanhood, as gender is at the core of our being. Because God created both male and female to be distinct individuals, we are not reflecting what He intends if we do not express our femininity. Destroying its beauty would prevent us from reflecting God's design.

## Putting an Ear to the Culture

I have the privilege of traveling around the country and gauging the pulse in women's hearts. As I detect the patterns of femininity portrayed in books, newspapers, and magazines, I see common threads of confusion about what it means to be a woman. Women are searching for meaning.

Many approach their femininity with a chip on their shoulders. They have been hurt by someone or by many, and they feel compelled to prove something. By constructing a thick wall around their emotions and by militantly defending their rights, they allow nothing to affect them. Unfortunately, our culture feeds this display of self-orientation. Such people appear to "have it together." But how many of these kinds of people exhibit a life full of joy and love?

Women sometimes search for fulfillment, significance, and importance in the natural places. And that's the problem. Maybe there is a preoccupation with physical beauty. Maybe there is a self-esteem search that leads to frantic busyness or a desire to have dominion over men. A woman with feminine splendor adds a supernatural aspect to the female formula that brings completeness and purpose. The God factor, when accurately defined, changes tension to a state of rest. We'll discuss this supernatural background in our next chapter.

A confused search for satisfaction often creates alienation and resistance within relationships. "My way is right; your way is wrong," we say. We seek to establish control through manipulation, but that is temporary relief. An acid tongue or subversive behavior may win an argument, but is true freedom realized?

This state of upheaval will continue to rule over gender identification until the end of time. There is an inner struggle going on of *Who am I?* and *How do I express who I am?* (It's called spiritual warfare.) In conversations, I notice expressions like powerlessness, sadness of soul, turmoil, need for freedom, feeling unappreciated, worthlessness, tension between children and career, need for monetary achievement, insecurity in regard to need for noteworthy status, feelings of being a parasite, being less than human, living life without using adult capabilities or intelligence, lacking purpose, missing parts, perceived inferiority, a mere pawn in a chess game, bored, unrewarded, and unfulfilled. And the list goes on.

# We Choose Our Response

Think of the old picture of how you see life: the glass is either half full or half empty. Those who view the glass as half full will see the joys, opportunities, and influence of expressing themselves as the feminine beings they are. This book is dedicated to the positive pleasure the female creature can experience when she expresses her complete self.

However, the half-empty viewers will continue to be destroyed by their victim orientation through their conscious and subconscious responses to life. Instead of focusing on having something, they look at what is missing. They are trying to find something else that will make them more whole, more complete. Instead of mirroring the heart of God, they feel limited and held back by what God didn't make them.

# And It's Not a Pretty Picture

When confused about gender roles, a woman commonly views herself as demeaned, possibly as a kind of slave. Instead of being free to give of herself, she feels the need to take everything she can get and to make her own way in life. (She's making her way, all right, and people are moving out of her way.) Taking "shots" at those closest to her is how she expels her venom of misery. You know what happens? In addition to hurting those closest to her, she hurts herself.

Oh, that she could only see how this gender confusion affects those around her. The pain in her heart not only contributes to her own poor mental health but eats away at the hearts of her husband, children, and associates as well.

In all of woman's search for more of "whatever" for herself, she may win a battle but lose the war. As Scripture says, "But many who are first will be last; and the last, first" (Matt. 19:30). Is she convinced? Not really.

## Hope through the Clouds

Aren't you glad we don't have to quit here? The darker the night, the brighter the light, it is said. And because confusion starts in the mind, we want to purge the old misconceptions and start playing new CDs of truth. "For as he thinks within himself, so he is" (Prov. 23:7). We can pray the prayer of intent, "Oh, God, help us save ourselves from ourselves."

Instead of being guided by passively accepted deception, we will be proactive. We will covenant to be like bankers in checking for counterfeit bills. Instead of dwelling on the negative features of bills, we will concentrate on what is good and right. We will immerse ourselves in the genuine. Only then will the counterfeit be obvious. Only then will we be able to discard it.

## Encouragement through Example

F. Carolyn Graglia graduated from prestigious Columbia University where she was an editor of the law review. After working in the Justice Department, she clerked on the Court of Appeals for the D.C. Circuit. Mrs. Graglia later left a promising career in a prominent Washington law firm to care for her husband and three children. She has written a book called *Domestic Tranquility: A Brief Against Feminism* in which she takes women through the clouds of confusion up into the blue sky of fulfillment through what she calls "awakened femininity."

> The woman who wishes to rear her children within a tra-ditional marriage, to whom contemporary feminism has been an implacable enemy, I call the "awakened Brunnhilde." Best-known from Richard Wagner's *The Ring of the Nibelung*, Brunnhilde is a warrior maiden who was transformed by her love for the hero Siegfried. The Brunnhilde I seek to defend is a woman who finds that the satisfactions of full-time commitment to being a wife and mother outweigh the rewards of pursuing a career. This realization is part of what I call her awakened femininity.
>
> But Brunnhilde's choice, according to societal consen-sus, is a sacrifice. It is viewed as a sacrifice because society has acquiesced in feminism's depiction of the homemaker's role as worthless, boring, unrewarding, unfulfilling, and incapable of using a woman's talents. Even those who sup-port this choice as being in children's best interest will speak of it as a sacrifice. For women like me, however, the sacrifice lies in precisely the opposite choice. It would have been a virtually unendurable sacrifice for me to leave my children with anyone (including my husband who, while possessing many virtues, was ill suited to a mother's role) in order to remain in the workplace.
>
> I have been happy in every period of my adult life: attending college and law school, practicing law, staying at home to raise a family, and creating a new life once my fam-ily responsibilities had largely ended. Yet those many years I spent as a mother at home from the birth of my first child until the last left for college were the best, the ones I would be least willing to have forgone. Feminists recount endless tales of women's oppression throughout the ages, but one of the greatest injustices to women is feminists' own success in

convincing society to treat as a sacrifice what for some women can be the most rewarding occupation of their lives.

By undermining the status and security of awakened Brunnhildes, contemporary feminism has inflicted unde-served injury upon many good women. And society itself has been weakened by its curtailing of women's domestic role, which contributes substantially—possibly more than any other single activity—to societal health and stability. All indicia of familial well-being demonstrate that our society was a significantly better place for families in the decade before the feminist revival—when the primary concerns of most mothers were their husbands, their chil-dren, and their home.[1]

## Rising above Confusion/Controversy

I'm aware that there is controversy about this topic and that some readers may have hostile feelings. As I write this book, I know there will be readers from every kind of background. If I were on my own, I might be intimidated. But because I have a higher power behind me, I have the con-fidence that I'm seeking to represent the Creator and Designer of life. I do tremble because I feel an awesome responsibility to do justice to God and to represent femininity through His lens.

As we work through this subject together, do remember our culture's need to be politically correct. A victim mentality can emerge within every realm, even the realm of femininity. The "What about me?" phrase is all too common from victims. The minorities (not the majority) feel entitled to equal status and even preferential treatment about so much. The polit-ically correct person wants the assurance that she is not left out.

## Regarding Singleness and/or Childlessness

One of my single and childless friend's favorite Scripture passages is this: " ' "For I know the plans that I have for you," declares the LORD, "plans

11

for welfare and not for calamity to give you a future and a hope. Then you will call upon Me and come and pray to Me, and I will listen to you. And you will seek Me and find Me, when you search for Me with all your heart"'" (Jer. 29:11–13).

Annie feels that she can depend on God for whatever He wills for her and that how she responds to life demonstrates her contentment as an unmarried and childless woman of God. Her attitude is that of Samuel, "'Speak, LORD, for Thy servant is listening'" (1 Sam. 3:9–10), and that of Isaiah, "'Here am I. Send me!'" (Isa. 6:8).

Annie also says, "It is God who makes me whole, not a job, a relationship on earth, or friends." John Piper reinforces this thought in *Recovering Biblical Manhood and Womanhood*: "We are persuaded from Scripture that masculinity and femininity are rooted in who we are by nature," he says. "They are not simply reflexes of a marriage relationship. Man does not become man by getting married. Woman does not become woman by getting married."[2]

Whether in biblical times or today, a woman's drive and ability to nurture moves her being. Pain, frustration, and questions only God can answer often linger when the womb is infertile.

Women are able to nurture people in every life situation, whether women are mothers or childless. Elisabeth Elliot says this about a childless woman: "She *can* have children! She may be a spiritual mother, as was Amy Carmichael, by the very offering of her singleness, transformed for the good of far more children than a natural mother may produce. All is received and made holy by the One to whom it is offered."[3]

# Single Mothering

The vast number of women that raise children alone is staggering. Incredible responsibility weighs on their shoulders, forcing them to fill roles beyond those designed for women. Single mothers may feel they have no time to devote to being a woman because they are too busy just trying to survive. In attempting to be both mother and father, such women often lose sight of their femininity. Yet their need for validation is great because they are spread so thin in accomplishing the work of multiple people.

Can a single mother handle the job . . . and how? She can only do so much, and the rest she must leave to our loving heavenly Father who promises to be "a father to the fatherless, a defender of widows" (Ps. 68:5, NIV). In my book, *Mom, You're Incredible* (I was raised by a single mom), I offer four ideas to help single moms: (1) Strive to have a positive attitude; (2) Refuse to give in to comparisons; (3) Never give up; and (4) Nurture your soul.[4]

# Order out of Chaos

Perfection will come when we enter heaven. In the meantime, God enables us to overcome our challenges and to be revitalized. The pieces can come together and we can sense order to this life, even though we may not have felt that order as we moved through life's clutter.

We have a wonderful calling to present the image of God by reflecting light as a woman. Each woman will do that as God has gifted her. We're unique. In the interests of time and space, we will explore here the life patterns common to most women. All women, however, are persons of God, created in His image for good works. And when we are not reflecting God's light in a true spirit of femininity, God's complete image is missing from humanity—or at least from our little corner of the world. May the passion of *Woman of Splendor* enable you to become brilliant in the basics for your maximum fulfillment. Living by God's principles can enliven your femininity.

CHAPTER 2

# *Biblical Authority*

Society gives many pictures of what it means to be a woman. How do we choose the right one? What rooting and grounding do we have behind our actions? Do we just follow what is right in our own eyes, or do we adhere to a standard? We need an authority, a base of stability. God wants to:

> grant [us], according to the riches of His glory, to be strengthened with power through His Spirit in the inner man; so that Christ may dwell in your hearts through faith; *and* that you, being rooted and grounded in love, may be able to comprehend with all the saints what is the breadth and length and height and depth, and to know the love of Christ which surpasses knowledge, that you may be filled up to all the fulness of God. (Eph. 3:16–19)

14

# No More Blindness

My friend Tracey has two daughters. Because she homeschools the girls, they missed the vision testing done in school. One day in church, one of the girls noticed her dad gaze at the screen up front and then look down to jot a note. She questioned him because it appeared that he might be reading something. Tracey and her husband discovered that neither girl could read the screen on the platform or the traffic signs outside.

The eye doctor confirmed that they were legally blind and needed corrective lenses. With glasses, suddenly everything around them came into focus. They were struck with the beauty that had been there all along.

If we are to live our lives in focus, we need to get fitted with God's lenses. Fuzzy confusion about femininity can be adjusted into understanding. We can have a totally different view if we "look through His glasses." There's a biblical authority which will grant us new perception as we choose to get fitted with God's lenses!

# You'll Love the Difference It Makes

It's exciting to me that I actually possess a pair of lenses that gets me into true levels of understanding. I don't have to wonder what femininity should look like or how I can be truly fulfilled. I can know. The Bible provides the pattern for femininity.

I love the way Ruth Myers thanks the Lord for enlightenment in life. She says, "Thank You that in Your Word I can see Your face and hear Your voice. I can discover Your will and Your patterns for living and serving. I can develop deeper faith and confidence. Thank You that the Holy Spirit inspired Your Word and uses it to enlighten and guide me and to change me more and more into Your image, from one degree of glory to another."[1]

We have godly insight available when we turn from our natural inclinations. But it often requires running from the way that feels right and good. "There is a way which seems right to a man, / But its end is the way of death" (Prov. 14:12). God's truth has felt like foolishness to so many.

15

"For the word of the cross is to those who are perishing foolishness, but to us who are being saved it is the power of God" (1 Cor. 1:18).

When we turn from the old way to the new, from self-absorption to a godly understanding, things start to make sense. "Whenever a man turns to the Lord, the veil is taken away. Now the Lord is the Spirit; and where the Spirit of the Lord is, there is liberty. But we all, with unveiled face beholding as in a mirror the glory of the Lord, are being transformed into the same image from glory to glory, just as from the Lord, the Spirit" (2 Cor. 3:16–18). The gray areas become more defined. Thank you, Lord.

# Following His Blueprint

I grew up with a heavy diet of the Scriptures, watching Mom read her Bible and live what she believed. If God said something, that settled it; we lived that way—happily, contentedly, confidently. We had every reason to trust God for everything because He was enough to meet our every need. We knew our heavenly Father was always with us and knew what was best for us. With His wisdom and power, He could accomplish any feat we needed.

We felt safe entrusting ourselves to a God who created us and knew what was best in every situation. We followed a God who always kept His promises and never changed. We believed we could be thankful for all the good things that we had, even when there was no money to buy soap to wash the clothes.

We lived in dire conditions. We had every earthly reason to fear and doubt. We lived in utter poverty, and yet my single mom with three children smiled at life, reminding us that God owns the cattle on a thousand hills and He always cares for us. When life-threatening situations surrounded us, we snuggled up close in our heavenly Father's embrace.

# Resting in God

Confidence to live with life's demands is developed through a trusting relationship with God. Because of the background of my early years, I feel blessed to be a woman. I have no need to challenge a holy God who has a plan for my life. Being close to my Refuge has enabled me to flourish as a woman, even when circumstances were less than desirable.

Through all the "stuff" we encounter along life's path, it is that immersion of our minds into God's thinking processes that causes us to exude a winsome aroma of a godly femininity. The pressure we feel to be more or better dissolves when we give ourselves to God. In the process, I realize I'm not self-made. I'm God-made.

Do you know what you feel like when you've eaten too much junk food? When you finally eat a healthy substantive meal, it feels so right. You might even remark, "I needed that." You relax more and feel contented. The same contentment comes when we trust God's authority rather than human wisdom. As we choose God over self, we commence a blossoming experience that exudes a pure fragrance.

# Purity

When the headwaters of our water supply are clear, we are free to drink confidently. While vacationing high in the Eagle Cap wilderness with my family, I was part of a group of hikers who reached the headwaters of a river. I filled my canteen and was ready to insert water purification tablets when I noticed the other hikers were confidently gulping the water straight from the stream.

"Relax," they said, laughing at my inexperience. "This is pure water. There's no one upstream to cause pollution."

The farther water flows from its source, the greater the likelihood of contamination. If people upstream toss waste into the water, the pure water becomes polluted. The same goes for our authority in life. "In the beginning was the Word, and the Word was with God, and the Word was God" (John 1:1). No one has access above the headwaters of God. If we choose to follow His stream, we are assured clarity of wisdom. If we choose a way other than God's, we can assume contamination. When women, who are created in God's image, are contaminated by following an ungodly stream, they reflect a contaminated view of God to the world.

# Begin with Truth

Geometry gives another illustration of how God's truth works. Do you remember those days in school when you needed to memorize geometry theorems? You started with true statements, or theorems. Then, because you had a stable fact with which to work, you could build a case on that truth. You continued to make logical conclusions with factual information. You determined the answer to problems because of the information deduced from the original theorem.

Biblical authority follows the principle of theorems. From its true statements, we can conclude other things that must be true because of our prior knowledge. This process teaches us how to think, make deductions, and draw conclusions. We can know what God expects of us by following after His heart. We can discern what paths are unsafe, unwise, and against God's will.

It would have been much easier if God had spelled everything out in chapters located all together on each subject. If it was easy to find sections of Scripture grouped together by topic with specific advice on how to be a helpmate, a nurturer, a relater, and a designer, it would be *too* easy. Instead, the Master Teacher gave us a whole Bible full of principles. From those principles, we can deduce all kinds of practical behavior that God expects of us. An immature person says, "God doesn't say what I have to be or do." A wise person searches for the principles and draws conclusions with persistent hard work.

This book is designed as a tool to help women discover God's intention for them. God is pleased as we find new appreciation in old truths.

# The Reservoir of Scripture

The following words from Scripture show the promises and reliability of God:

> Those who seek the LORD understand all things. (Prov. 28:5)

> We labor and strive, because we have fixed our hope on the living God. (1 Tim. 4:10)

"Therefore everyone who hears these words of Mine, and acts upon them, may be compared to a wise man, who built his house upon the rock. And the rain descended, and the floods came, and the winds blew, and burst against that house; and yet it did not fall, for it had been founded upon the rock. And everyone who hears these words of Mine, and does not act upon them, will be like a foolish man, who built his house upon the sand. And the rain descended, and the floods came, and the winds blew, and burst against that house; and it fell, and great was its fall." (Matt. 7:24–27)

For you know what commandments we gave you by the authority of the Lord Jesus. . . . He who rejects this is not rejecting man but the God who gives His Holy Spirit to you. (1 Thess. 4:2, 8)

All Scripture is inspired by God and profitable for teaching, for reproof, for correction, for training in righteousness; that the man of God may be adequate, equipped for every good work. (2 Tim. 3:16–17)

We have the prophetic word made more sure, to which you do well to pay attention as to a lamp shining in a dark place. . . . But know this first of all, that no prophecy of Scripture is a matter of one's own interpretation, for no prophecy was ever made by an act of human will, but men moved by the Holy Spirit spoke from God. (2 Pet. 1:19–21)

ALL FLESH IS LIKE GRASS,
AND ALL ITS GLORY LIKE THE FLOWER OF GRASS.
THE GRASS WITHERS,
AND THE FLOWER FALLS OFF,
BUT THE WORD OF THE LORD ABIDES FOREVER."
(1 Pet. 1:24–25)

The assurance we need will come from our acquired reservoir of God's Word. Reminders are important. Otherwise, we are influenced by other sources. Our thinking becomes cloudy all too easily, leaving us vulnerable to disagree with God, choosing self over God.

# "Choose for Yourselves Today"[2]

When we buy a product, we receive an instruction book to learn to use the purchase most effectively. When we receive life, God issues a Book for maximum effectiveness. We have the option of using the guidebook or not.

We may decide which authority to live by. If you choose God as your authority, as I have, we will be proceeding together on the same foundational level of understanding. Unified in purpose, we'll be able to sing the words of one of my favorite songs: "I Am Finding Out the Greatness of Thy Loving Heart."

As we respond to principles of truth, we respond to God, not some human idea. God is always waiting to talk when we have questions and/or disagreements, so do seek Him and His mind on any matter. Biblical authority gives us confidence to become comfortable with our created design.

# Differences between Masculine and Feminine

My husband and I have been married thirty-three years. Before the wedding we noticed plenty of differences between us, but we were excited about uniting to create that perfect blend. We're not coffee drinkers, but we now realize that the idea of "a perfect blend" should be reserved for those who appreciate that unique cup of ground beans rather than applied to some married couple. Perfection is reserved for heaven.

This reminds me of a line our pastor often used years ago: "Fellowship with the saints above, oh, that will be glory. As for the saints below, that's another story."

Our differences don't have to be devastating if we will only learn and grow through them. Oh, that we will search for the pearls of wisdom that unleash our individual magnificence. I don't think God ever intended for us to quit working on uniting these differences, and it does require our life work.

The differences between Stu and me have been more than amusing. At times I've thought God must have an interesting sense of humor, putting two people together who feel as if they've come from different planets. *How could he think like this?* I'd say to myself. Or, *Why would he even consider doing that?* Sometimes I felt that he was being insensitive to what was important to me. Other times, I'm sure I failed to affirm his manhood.

Differences between the sexes are extensive and leave us in a quandary until we sort them out. As we take the time to understand each gender, we gain new freedom to act on our God-given femininity.

# Oil and Water

Does a man's behavior take you by surprise occasionally? It can almost be entertaining when we compare a woman's definition of "right" to what we observe in a man. After all, how can anyone buy a good-looking outfit without trying it on? And who ever heard of buying the first item you see without looking for something better—just in case? Instead of getting angry, we need to relax and chuckle our way through the differences. We might be surprised at how God ordered all this.

Have you tried to mix oil and water? It doesn't work until you mix other ingredients with it. If a cake had oil and vanilla as the only ingredients, it simply wouldn't be a cake. But if you add flour and a rising agent, some sweetener and a few other variables, you can create a delicious product.

Good cooks find just the right combination of carefully chosen ingredients. It takes wisdom, time, determination, and work. In your experience of combining differences, you may need some additional elements to get the kind of product you're hoping for. There's nothing like that seasoned cook who learns over time how to blend just the right ingredients.

# Real Life Happens

In the kitchen of life we see people popping quick options into microwaves, hoping for some gourmet marriage experience. They may get by, but they won't appreciate a great lifetime adventure.

Other couples who marry without knowledge of gender differences and have no inclination to work hard don't stay married. They split up in frustration, convinced they married the "wrong" person. The high divorce rate and the number of unhappy relationships alert us to the presence of gender differences. A successful marriage must be one of the hardest assignments to accomplish. Because the Creator designed us as individuals and gave man and woman to each other, we need to labor to maximize His intentions.

# Can You Identify?

Being the mother of three wonderful sons, I was a minority in a fraternity. For thirty-two years the testosterone flowed through our home like rivers overflowing after a rainstorm. I needed to catch my girl connections elsewhere. Now that all my sons are married, I have some new feminine relationships with my daughters-in-law, which I'm really enjoying. Three girls are a fun addition to balance our family scales. Though I would never have traded any of my men, the new daughters enrich all of our lives with that graceful feminine side.

Maybe you can identify with some of these differences. My men never enjoyed shopping. In typical guy fashion, they went into a store only when they wanted something. When we found it, we got it and left—no looking around or shopping for other options. That would not be their idea of a good time. They focus on one thing at a time.

The boys loved to wrestle and take each other down. I was always worried they would hit their heads on the coffee table or go through a window. In their active play outside, I was always afraid the lace-leaf maple tree would lose one or two of its major branches. Sure enough, it happened, but the boys survived. They must have been tougher than the tree!

One of the boys did walk through a full-length piece of glass when the rest of us were walking through the door beside it. As a male, he was concentrating on one thing—going straight ahead into that building. The glass was so clean and his mind was not focused on anything but the task of getting where he was going. Women can process multiple situations simultaneously. Guys often concentrate on doing only one thing at a time.

A friend recently told me about what happened when her husband was broiling some open-face sandwiches. She asked him to put food in the cat's dish while he was standing there.

He got rather flustered and responded, "I'm busy. I can't do that."

He really couldn't do two things at once. A man's brain is wired much differently than a woman's, as we'll see a bit later.

We all know that a woman is capable of talking on the phone, stirring the pot, caring for a clinging child, watching those open-face sandwiches under the broiler, and giving a little food to the cat while she's taking notes for the directions she needs to get to a party tonight.

Yesterday at the store, I gave the clerk a few dollar bills for goods I purchased. As I looked for the correct change, he said, "I wait for the ladies 'cause they always give me the coins too. The guys only pay with bills."

Do you have containers of change at your house because your husband also only pays with bills? That issue is rather insignificant, but things get more serious when we become angry over other kinds of differences. When our love dwindles because of this anger, we obviously need to pursue an understanding about our differences.

# I Can't Figure It Out

My husband, Stu, says this in his book *Tender Warrior*,

> A woman is more delicate. She is the fine china, not the stoneware. She is a finely tuned sports car, not a '66 Chevy pickup with mud flaps. She is more fragile, more sensitive. She has a more precisely adjusted sensory ability, especially in terms of relationships. A woman is more alert to what is happening in her environment. We men need to grasp the significance of these realities and live with them wisely.[1]

Regardless of who we are, understanding differences is an ongoing need. You might smile as you see the words from Freud, the well-known "student of sex" from the past. In his seventy-seventh year, after most of his ideas had passed from theory into dogma, the so-called father of psychiatry admitted to his diary that he didn't understand women. "What do women want?" he wrote. "God, God, what do they want?"[2]

# We're Equal but Different

We've only just begun to look at how men and women are different. It seems obvious to many that we are unique from each other and yet the debate goes on. The complementarian view says that we are equal but have different functions. Those functions are different because God wired and blessed us differently. The egalitarian view says equality is sameness, which eliminates any unique male leaders. More is going on here than word games. Scripture is being redefined in the latter view.

God looks at men and women as equal. "There is neither Jew nor Greek, there is neither slave nor free man, there is neither male nor female; for you are all one in Christ Jesus" (Gal. 3:28). The Scriptures go on and on telling how we are both saved through grace, coheirs of grace, both indwelt with the Spirit of God, not to be independent of each other, both privileged to have access to God through prayer. God created us equal and He created us different—what a paradox.

# Mind the Gap (as the British say)

You may remember in the movie *Rocky* where Rocky said of Adrian, "I've got gaps. She's got gaps. Together we got no gaps."

There's solid truth there. Each person has strengths and weaknesses. Put them together, and they complement each other. They fill each other's gaps. No wonder so many opposites are attracted to one another. In general, the male and female gaps are intended to be closed as we unite in marriage.

As you approach the underground subway tracks in England you see the sign "Mind the Gap." There is a space between the train's car and the loading platform, so you must be careful to pay attention to the gap to avoid trouble. God needs us to "mind the gaps" in our relationships or those differences could divide us. There's much to learn in keeping us from falling in the gap.

# Four Kinds of Differences

One way to make difficult things more easily understood is to break them into categories or to set them in groups. My husband and I have studied gender differences and believe there are four categories that distinguish men and four for women.

## Life Categories

At the end of this chapter, on page 33, is a chart from my husband's book *Four Pillars of a Man's Heart*.³ This chart shows the man's categories graphically presented as: *king, warrior, mentor,* and *friend*. The intentions of each category are given: to provide, to protect, to teach, and to connect. If any one category gets out of balance in either direction, the chart lists the consequential behavior.

Women's roles can be broken into four categories as well. The four facets of femininity are: *helpmate, nurturer, relater,* and *designer*. Each category also has an accompanying intention or purpose: to partner, to develop, to connect, to beautify. You'll see these concepts at a glance through studying the diagram on page 34. When you want to take your study to another level, you might consider a book that is somewhat technical but very faithful to the Bible—*Recovering Biblical Manhood and Womanhood* by John Piper and Wayne Grudem.⁴

## Body Uniqueness

An anatomy student would need many volumes to present the physical differences between men and women, but the following short list can begin our understanding.

- Men and women differ in every cell of their bodies.
- Women have greater constitutional vitality, perhaps because of chromosome difference.

- The sexes differ in their basal metabolism—that of a woman being normally lower than that of a man.
- In physiological functions, women have several very important ones totally lacking in men—menstruation, pregnancy, and lactation. All of these influence behavior and feelings. Women have more different hormones than do men. The same gland behaves differently in the two sexes—the woman's thyroid is larger and more active; it enlarges during pregnancy but also during menstruation. It makes her more prone to goiter; provides resistance to cold; and is associated with a smooth skin, a relatively hairless body, and a thin layer of subcutaneous fat, which are elements in the concept of personal beauty.
- Women's blood contains more water (20 percent fewer red cells). Since red cells supply oxygen to the body cells, she tires more easily and is more prone to faint.
- A woman's heart beats more rapidly (80 beats vs. 72 for men); blood pressure (10 points lower than men) varies from minute to minute, but she has much less tendency to high blood pressure—at least until after menopause.[5]
- The woman's immunization system is more complex. She produces more immunoglobulin M. Her estrogen protects her from heart disease.[6]
- Many women experience PMS, which, of course, is exclusively female.

## Brain Responses

We'll work through this more in chapter 16, "Expression Made through Details." When we focus on emotional/relational patterns, we'll discover that woman is much more verbal than man. We will pursue this more when dealing with the section "Relater Meant to Connect." Woman is more feelings-oriented, and man is more logical and matter-of-fact. Woman tends to use both sides of her brain simultaneously, and man usually uses one side or the other. More issues than you might expect stem from the differences that are in your head, and I don't mean perceived as opposed to real. *Time* magazine reported that there are "subtle neurological differences between the sexes both in the brain's structure and in its functioning."[7]

The woman is relationally strong; the man is task oriented. One of my daughters-in-law wanted some attention from her husband, so she attached a stick-on note to her blouse that said, "I'm a task, do me."

I thought her idea was brilliant. Men are wired to pursue tasks that they see listed in their daily planners. And if we should be listed as some job to do, they just might see more reason to pursue a deeper relationship with us.

One of the biggest struggles in most marriages is the difference we have regarding sex. As Stu and I taught the FamilyLife Marriage Conference for years, we discovered that one big area of need was helping partners understand their sexual differences. Men and women differ in attitude, stimulation, needs, sexual response, and with orgasm.[8]

Men are more physically oriented and less sensitive, and again, they forge ahead on task. Women want to linger with conversation and tenderness to be adequately prepared for a fulfilling physical expression through sex. The woman's focus lies on relational wholeness. She likes the touch, and yet his stimulation comes more naturally by sight. The man's general pursuit of sex could be likened to the microwave, whereas the woman is more the Crock-Pot design with a need to simmer long and slow. Isn't it interesting that God planned these large differences to meld us together?

I love the way Gary Smalley, in his book *For Better or for Best*, compared the psychological makeup of woman to man. He drew a comparison using the butterfly to the buffalo. The butterfly has this keen sensitivity to the slightest breeze, fluttering above the ground for the panoramic awareness of life. It reacts with swiftness toward anything that might hurt it. And if a tiny pebble were taped to its wing, it could be severely injured and eventually die.

As for the buffalo, he is rough, calloused, and doesn't react to a breeze. He is not affected by a 30-mph wind. He is not aware of small flowers and might even crush them unknowingly. He is not sensitive to changes in his environment, and a pebble on his back wouldn't be noticed.[9] Are you smiling with recognition?

Dee Brestin described the differences this way: "Women suggest and share and men command and report."[10] It's part of that relational vs. logical style we're born with. She wants to feel the details, and he wants to get to the bottom line. All this is why women say, "He doesn't have enough feelings," and men say, "She's too emotional."

## General Needs

Look around at your friends or check the polls. You'll generally find similarities with men and women's needs at large. Willard Harley says that women most frequently list their needs in this order:

He meets her need for
- affection—hugs, kisses, words, cards, flowers, gifts, and common courtesies. It's the environment that matters.
- intimate conversation at the feeling level. He listens.
- honesty and openness by looking her in the eye and telling her what he really thinks.
- financial support.
- commitment by putting the family first.

The man has a different list of his needs and a different order.

She meets his need for
- sexual fulfillment by becoming an excellent sexual partner.
- recreational companionship by developing mutual interests.
- beauty by keeping herself attractive.
- domestic support by managing the home.
- admiration and respect by understanding his value and achievements more than anyone else.[11]

# How Is the Devil Involved?

We don't think much about the devil in regard to male-female differences. But Satan's negative presence and activity affect us more than we would like to think. Becoming aware of his methods can help us do battle against his force. He attacks us by wanting to:

**DESTROY . . .**

1. God's image, which is male and female. (He wants to tear us apart.)
2. our differentness, how we complement one another. (If that is destroyed, the picture of God is absent.)
3. marriage and love. (He wants to destroy families and the people who make them work.)

**PROMOTE . . .**

1. frustration with differences. (He wants us to be angry with each other.) "Frustration is a warning signal that I am not appreciating God's creation design of gender differences to bring completeness and balance to the home and church."[12]
2. independence, self-potential. (He turns us from responsibility.)
3. rejection of God. (He promotes selfishness and human domination rather than submission, as a dominant wife confuses the children. The children don't know whom to follow.)
4. confusion about equality. (He wants us to think that equality equals sameness.)
5. victim mentality. (He wants us to blame God for our pain and frustration.)
6. deception. (He will mislead us through vain human philosophies.)
7. destruction. (It's his nature to destroy, in the name of being equal and powerful.)

# What Do We Do with Differences?

May these guidelines be helpful in our pilgrimage.

1. Realize that differences exist.
2. Accept them. Differentness is OK. It is good. Develop a new level of contentment.
3. Rehearse the facts: God designed this. In marriage we were made for each other. We belong to each other. We each have our responsibilities. Be aware of differences so as not to be taken by surprise.
4. Allow differences to be assets. Appreciate the value of each one. Give grace. Learn to find the good in the way others do things. Don't hold the man hostage until he conforms to our way. Give and take with him.
5. Relinquish expectations. "When we hold to the expectation that a man must succeed in every regard every time, we drive that man further from us. As you respond to your man with encouragement, forgiveness, and a firm belief in him, you will have a great impact on his life."[13] Life will be sweeter.
6. Try a new response. Change your approach. (Try saying, "I like it when you _____." "It means a lot to me when _____." Or, "I love to see you _____.")
7. Be responsibly flexible to incorporate differences; use them to actually meet needs.

# Awareness Elevates Your Quality of Life

The following advice comes from a married woman whose twin is a man. Joan Shapiro is a medical doctor with male patients and is a counselor to both men and women. "When trying to understand a man, and in trying to have the relationship with him that we so want, we have to learn to read his signals from his perspective, using his language, to know what he really feels and means. . . . We are all concerned with the same 'stuff,' we just have different solutions for dealing with it."[14]

31

If you have little boys, please encourage them in the way of maleness. And if you have little girls, they must be escorted into the feminine way at every opportunity. To do otherwise warps their sexual orientation and leaves them marred for life.

Belittling differentness as something strange will haunt your future generations through deviant behavior. One family I know saw major destruction take place in three sons. The mom had wanted girls, not boys. She insisted on pushing the boys into feminine patterns from which they never recovered. It is a sad story we must not repeat in our homes.

One way of doing things is not superior over the other. Because of "differentness," definitions of "right" and "best" don't apply. We are different by the Creator's design. We each have the utmost value and importance. The sooner we comprehend this lofty concept of designed differences, the better our attitudes will be toward one another and the more we will love God's way. Awareness of gender differences not only earns you an A in relationships but also labels you as a master diplomat for your expertise in dealing with others.

⁂

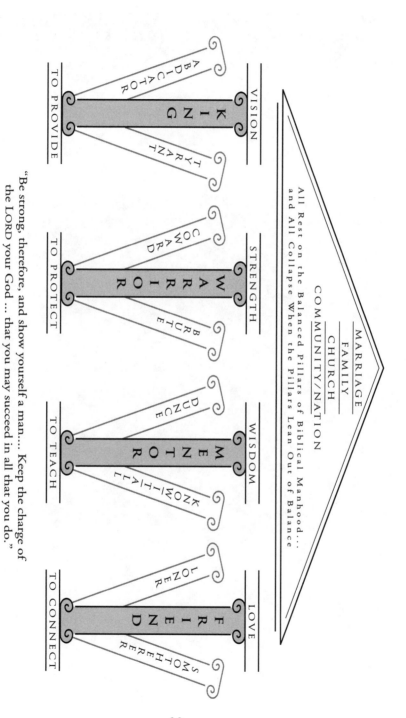

TO PROVIDE — VISION

KING

ABCDEFG

MZARTY

TO PROTECT — STRENGTH

WARRIOR

COWARD

BRUTE

TO TEACH — WISDOM

MENTOR

DUNCE

MANIPULATOR

TO CONNECT — LOVE

FRIEND

LONER

SMOTHERS

COMMUNITY/NATION

CHURCH

FAMILY

MARRIAGE

All Rest on the Balanced Pillars of Biblical Manhood...
and All Collapse When the Pillars Lean Out of Balance

"Be strong, therefore, and show yourself a man.... Keep the charge of the LORD your God ... that you may succeed in all that you do."

1 KINGS 2:2–3

"Four mighty ones are in every man." —William Blake

33

# The Jewel of Femininity

adorn
enhance

**DESIGNER**
*to beautify*

**HELPMATE**
*to partner*

support
encourage

*darken* *destroy*
degrade dominate
dismantle diminish

*distract* *demolish*
disengage deprive
distance discourage

**RELATER**
*to connect*

**NURTURER**
*to develop*

link
comfort

foster
empower

© 1999 Linda Weber

## CHAPTER 4

# The Jewel of Femininity

*Y*ears ago I worked on many stitchery projects. First, I chose the piece to be stitched. Then, I started collecting the materials to incorporate. Many, many hours went into putting all those different colors and types of threads together. I got excited as the design emerged. As I have been preparing to share numerous details with you about femininity, I have gotten excited as well. I love seeing the pieces come together that will give you something concrete to hang on the walls of your heart.

Those pieces can help you feel validated as a woman. So, what is femininity? Many women ask, "Who am I?" and "How do I function best?" The essence of woman is a matter of gender—who God created us to be, besides how He intends for us to be fulfilled. Stay with me as we capture her four primary parts along with her myriad of functions.

# Putting Parts Together

I like order. I like to see how things fit together. In junior high, I loved diagramming sentences (much to the amazement of my friends). I couldn't get enough of it. Seeing how all those parts of the sentence related to the others fascinated me. When I knew who or what that sentence was all about, I knew what we were talking about. When I learned the verbs, I could see the relationship between the subject and its activity as I placed each on the diagram. The sentences became alive as I added the descriptive details.

As the parts of our femininity start coming together, our awareness will energize us. New appreciation will excite us as the lights turn on and the bells ring with the understanding of God's intention. We can thrive in our relationships as women when we follow these words: "If we walk in the light as He Himself is in the light, we have fellowship with one another" (1 John 1:7).

# The Right Ingredients

Years ago at my bridal shower, the women brought their favorite recipes for my growing collection. My mother went through them all very carefully and corrected one item that was obviously wrong. The woman had written "1 cup of salt" instead of "1 teaspoon." Being totally unfamiliar with the kitchen scene back then, I probably would have added 1 cup of salt to the dish. That would have created a disaster. We must have the right ingredients and the proper balance of each to ensure a desired goal.

So what are the ingredients that make up God's design for femininity? Our culture is obsessed with what we can see. It's hard for many to go below the surface and consider the foundational-type ingredients. But these are every bit as real and substantive as the ones that are easily visible.

As I listen to women, I hear them express a need for personal power and self-definition. They want to feel like a woman and be all they can be. Women need affirmation, and of course God wants us to be affirmed. But is there more within the divine framework of God's design? The right ingredients are those God chooses. Then the lady who "receives" her design package is set up to reflect God's light. As she activates "the right ingredients," she fulfills her femininity.

As a woman comes to appreciate her ability to reflect light, she can exude an unexplainable contentment in knowing Christ and His plan. In the process she will be living out Scripture—"I can do all things through Him who strengthens me" (Phil. 4:13), and "godliness actually is a means of great gain, when accompanied by contentment" (1 Tim. 6:6).

# We're Like the Diamond

Women are like diamonds. No two are alike. We're valued as precious. We have a wide range of transparency and color. (We wear a lot of hats.) We actually conduct heat. (We do provide warmth.) God takes that chunk of carbon and cuts it to refine us through numerous processes necessary to achieve incredible beauty. It's when we have been cut that our fire and brilliance shine brightest. (The diamond-cutting process is painful but adds to our beauty and brings glory to God.)

The final step of the cutting is the polishing, which consists of forming the facets on the finished stone. We are most valuable as we are reflecting more light from the Source. Every angle displays a new look, a new design. And interestingly enough, the blemishes we have affect our value.

We need to rid ourselves of any grime that hinders reflection. Maybe we must put our diamond into the cleaning solution (God's Word) and get a thorough cleaning to make peace with our past.

Are any facets clouded with anger that disguises your beauty? I encourage you to let your gifts be seen through the various facets of your femininity as you explore, discover, and realize all your potential to reflect light. That discovery process will help you to "set sail on your own voyage to a new land with fertile opportunities. Courage and patience will see you through until the seeds of your gifts take root, sprout above the surface, and bear fruit."[1]

# The Four Facets in the Jewel of Femininity

Examine the diagram on page 34. Notice that there are four facets to the jewel: *helpmate, nurturer, relater,* and *designer.* See how each facet has a corresponding purpose or intention: to partner, to develop, to connect, and to beautify.

## Helpmate Meant to Partner

In Genesis, we see that God planned for a woman and man to come together. Without this marriage union, there would be no ongoing human race. God designed woman to be a partner to her husband, to help and support him, to complement him and his abilities, and to adapt to him. A good wife is a "helpmate suitable."

We will refer to many portions of Scripture to help in understanding this. Strong examples of God's intention for the helpmate will be given to aid in putting these principles into shoe leather. We will deal with commitment and submission besides speaking to a tendency to rebel against these patterns. Since you are a partner in marriage, tools for building a marriage will be offered.

You will be challenged with the seriousness of your vow. It is more than a good idea to get a strong grip on the personal responsibility involved. The effect of your life as a "helpmate suitable" is indeed far-reaching, both now and for generations to come.

What about the unmarried woman? There are exceptions to many "rules" but the presentation here is designed for a general audience. A single person can practice the principles of being a helpmate suitable by showing loyalty, support, encouragement, purity, commitment, and submission to those around her. These qualities are needed in subordinate relationships in the office, church, and community.

## Nurturer Meant to Develop

God has designed the woman physically and psychologically to nurture. Her body is part of that process—"as a nursing mother tenderly cares for her own children" (1 Thess. 2:7). The Bible pictures women not only as providing sustenance for the child at the breast but also as being close at hand to comfort and provide emotional support. Her ready help aids in the maturation process and is essential for children's healthy development.

The principles of nurturing don't just apply to mothers. I have numerous friends who diligently work at nurturing various nonrelatives. It is a woman's nature to nurture, and she can find suitable avenues to pursue whether or not she has children.

As we appreciate the opportunity of the woman to reflect light to future generations through the skillful nurturing of children (the most obvious nurturing), we can agree with these words of Carol Brazo: "This is the picture of a woman's life over the long haul, the impossible made possible by taking tiny steps. The routines of life enforcing the miraculous. Ordinary jobs becoming sacred, holy occupations."[2]

We'll see how nurturing happens and fill in some blind spots that frequently keep us from the goals we thought we were working for. And if we're in the process of nurturing nearly grown children, are we activating the healthy biblical principle of letting go?

## Relater Meant to Connect

The feminine creature is a relational genius. She connects with verbal means, but the tie to making things happen lies in her being at the hub of every circle. You may not have realized your value as a hub until now. It's like almost any appliance: until it breaks, you don't know how important it is. This section helps home managers and hubs of any circle stand taller with renewed pride.

We've seen Mary praised over the years for her spiritual devotion as opposed to Martha's busywork. Consider Jami Lyn's reflection on this.

> I always feel like Martha gets an unfair bad rap—like all women should be a Mary. But I don't think that's what Jesus would say. I think he liked visiting Lazarus because Martha made him feel welcome and comfortable and because he loved her cooking. I don't think he asked for reservations for the Last Supper by accident. He didn't forget the calendar. I

think Martha was taking care of it. (She lived nearby and was dependable and talented in this area.) Martha did need to be reminded to slow down and sit at Jesus' feet. It's a good reminder for us all, even in the midst of exercising our gifts. I just want to be a Martha with Mary's spirit and timing.

Another of my daughters-in-law called one evening and related a difficult time she was facing. She shared how one of her friends responded to her so much like a biblical Martha. My daughter-in-law said, "She was not formal or technical. She showed immediate identification and was entirely accepting of my feelings. She wanted to help in prayer. She respected my feelings—was very receiving and accepting. She gave support without having expectations."

When we are tired and unable to hold up under the pressures we face, wouldn't it be nice to have a Martha nearby? You have the raw material to be a Martha, a true relater meant to connect.

## Designer Meant to Beautify

Women like to beautify themselves and their surroundings. We can't talk about femininity without appreciating the wonderful female body. It's not supposed to be our focus but should be recognized with honor and respect. Because God created us with such flair, we need to do justice to our bodies.

The older conservative Christian crowd may not believe we should give time to this subject. Yet the whole counsel of God urges us to respect ourselves as our Lord would and to keep things in balance. Young girls tend to obsess over their appearance. It would be wonderful if church leaders promoted Christian charm courses for girls to teach them how to bring the beautification of self into balance with the blossoming of the inner woman. When feminine charm is used to benefit others as God designed, femininity is beautiful.

As women age, we learn to accept our bodies and we turn our focus toward inner beauty. When our bodies go through menopause, we can make leaps toward greater maturity.

All life is a struggle for maturity through predictable events and unpredictable crises. We cannot afford to jump over any of its stages. They are all good, even the infamous midlife crisis, a time to evaluate and be renewed. Dr. Theo Bovet, a Swiss doctor, called menopause "femininity lost and then refound in a more wonderful way." In Africa a woman is considered a bearer of wisdom when she has completed menopause. It is the process by which a woman integrates all the stages of life.[3]

Nesting is an inborn quality of women. We want to make our surroundings beautiful and comfortable. A pastor's wife moved with her husband and three children from one state to another. Wanting to sell their old house quickly, they decided to leave it fully furnished. They rented a small apartment and moved. "I didn't have anything to bring but some basement furniture," she said. "We just put mattresses on the floor and lived with the bare necessities."

Alone in a bland apartment all day, this woman became depressed. "I was completely supportive of my husband and agreed with all our arrangements, so I was surprised. Looking back, I believe I experienced a sense of grief and loss in leaving friends, but I'm sure the ugly apartment was part of the problem."

Learning how to transform fragments into beauty is a means of reflecting the light God placed in our souls. Again, I think our little girls would be served well if we developed their abilities to create pleasing atmospheres. Life takes place in settings. Comfortable and beautiful surroundings facilitate the work of life in the heart and mind.

All this beautifying is done through an expression of details. God created woman to appreciate and pursue these details. Women like to put the little pieces together, whereas this doesn't appeal to many men. God uses each of the four facets of women to reflect light from Himself.

# Diamonds in the Rough

Think about that little house down the street that is a diamond in the rough. Weeds cover the yard, and the exterior needs some paint and a few repairs. The appearance prevents most buyers from realizing the real gem this house truly is. It also enables a smart buyer to purchase the house for less than a comparable house that is well kept. Diamonds and houses pass from rough to valuable as some careful work is applied. The old things have to be ripped out or dug up. Yes, it'll require diligence, but it will shine and offer value beyond expectation.

What will happen to us if we decide not to allow God to polish us?

One woman I know keeps her diamonds—both literal and figurative ones—hidden away. Although she owns several expensive gems, she keeps them locked in a safe. She's ninety and has never worn the jewelry—at least as far as I know. She never shows off their brilliance to anyone for fear that someone might steal or lose them.

She keeps the brilliance of her personality locked away too. She reaches out to no one. She has few visitors. She rarely smiles. Perhaps she's afraid she might "use up" her goodness, or maybe she wants to safeguard the jewel of her personality from being bumped or hurt by others.

The paradox of God's design for women is that the more we give to others, even though it is a risk, the more we receive from God and the more brightly the splendor of our womanhood shines.

Oh, that we will enjoy taking our diamond to the shop to be polished by God. God wants us to reflect His beauty, but first we must have our filmy coverings removed. "He who began a good work in you will perfect it until the day of Christ Jesus" (Phil. 1:6). Then we will shine. We can sing, "Let the Beauty of Jesus Be Seen in Me."

With a big picture of God, we will not feel limited because we are women. Instead, we will understand the expanse of our opportunities as women. There is power in the Book that gives hope. If you have obstacles in life, you can be enabled to overcome. Joni Eareckson Tada, who despite paralysis ministers to others, said, "Remember that you can learn to delight in every obstacle God places in your path. Limitations force us to yield, to abandon ourselves to our creator, God. And when we do, his creativity flows!"[4]

Enjoy the woman God created you to be. Find opportunities to express the full beauty of your femininity to others.

❧

# PART 2

# Facet #1:

# Helpmate Meant to Partner

## CHAPTER 5

# A Helpmate Suitable

*Y*ears ago when we were looking to buy our first house, the realtor told us that there were three factors to consider: location, location, location.

Last week as Dr. Earl and Ruth Radmacher were staying in our home, Dr. "R" made the same kind of statement regarding the subject he is teaching our people at church. He said, "When it comes to hermeneutics (the art or the science of interpretation of literature), there are three factors you must pursue when determining meaning: context, context, and context."

When it comes to reflecting light as a helpmate, there are three factors that determine how we gleam as a woman: attitude, attitude, and attitude. In Proverbs 23:7 we are told: As we think, so we are.

What you think will influence your attitude. The thesaurus says your *attitude* is your posture, stance, disposition, and your outlook. It is your state of mind or sentiment regarding another. What you think affects your attitude, which in turn affects your actions. Everything that happens in our homes is colored by how we think about being a helpmate. Our attitude affects all of life just as perfume permeates every corner of a room.

A lofty concept of being a helpmate is poignantly portrayed in letters I received from Carolyn, who later married our oldest son, Kent. Carolyn's words speak a message of a good heart attitude.

Although the words from her letters are intensely personal, the tenderness with which she shares and the biblical truth she mentions are good reminders for all of us. Carolyn gave me permission to allow you to peek into her heart.

> Dearest Mom,
>
> Kent's love, as I'm reminded of again and again, just covers me. It is like God's love. Mom, Kent brings one closer to God all the time. It's as though the Lord, in His great kindness and mercy, has placed Kent in my life as an earthly embodiment of this love for us. There is no other single human being I respect more, strive to better myself for more, think about more, and dearly love more than Kent. I just want so badly to give him the joy and peace of mind and heart he gives me. I pray always that I will be a good wife to him—that I will anticipate his needs before he must even ask, that I'll be what he needs even before he realizes the need himself.
>
> When I was little, I used to believe in white knights on great steeds, in good princes with hearts of gold, in dragon-slayers and heroes. As I grew older, I didn't become so cynical that I lost complete sight of this, but I did bury such "dreams" away—they were too dangerous to believe in because such heroes could not truly exist. But they do exist, modeled in Christ, they do. I have learned so many things in learning about my faith, among them just what reflection relationships in our lives are of His love for us. The ultimate of all these is marriage. Your eldest son is a hero. He saved me from myself and he saved me constantly, through the giving of himself, through his incarnation into what it is like to be me, to assume my

burdens and relieve my worries. My relationship with God is, like anyone else's ultimately, a personal one. But Kent has translated it for me into the dynamics of living it, of putting it in action. I have been in love with your son for a long time. So much so, I had resigned myself to his not ever loving me back. If need be I would rather love him at a distance than anyone else up close. But, by the grace of God, he does love me. My heart still marvels at that. There isn't anything I wouldn't do for him. God help anyone who crosses him or tries to! I'm his bulldog and his butterfly. But most of all, I just want to serve him. I just want to do all I can to glorify him. I truly believe that the best way I can live my life to God's glory is to live it in glorifying Kent Weber. It may sound silly, but I mean it with every fiber of my being when I say it gives me more honor to iron a single shirt of his than to teach at a million Oxfords. I'm not immaturely, or what they would call "blindly," in love—for I see. Boy, do I see! To make him happy makes me happy. He is everything to me, and I am everything to him. You have raised a hero—you have raised, lovingly, someone I barely dared to believe existed. Bless you always, always for that, and know you have my undying respect and love for all that you both are.

Kent, I fear, sometimes worries a little that I may be resentful or one day regret giving up "all I have" (professionally) for him. He sometimes intimates such. We have to work on him here. You so kindly offer your help to me—perhaps you could help me in this way? Help him to see that all is worthless for me without him. I feel like a finely trained athlete, a racehorse at the gate, an edgy runner at the starting line—I have been trained my whole life for him and am now ready to Go. To run the race with him, but to help him in every suitable way along the way. The rest is superfluous. Sure, I have many "things" here in a place I've worked very hard to reach, but I am miserable without Kent because nothing else exists even remotely worthy of investing in. I so want him to rest easy in the knowledge of that.

*That my greatest honor comes from bearing his name, not the initials of a degree; of bearing his children, not producing an article or holding a position. The only position I want is the one by his side, from his side. Your son is a treasure. Any true intelligence I own is precisely because I know his worth. Of all the things that Oxford gave me and could have given me, it brought me to Kent Weber. Life began there. And I'm having so much fun with that! It's just all so decadent! Wow!*

*Well, I guess all that is to say, I'm one happy camper! Please know I couldn't love or cherish Kent any more than I do, and I look forward to a life of growing in Christ with and for him. You are hero-raising people . . . I am overjoyed to be accepted as your daughter. I love you incredibly and cannot wait to see you . . . what a noble calling to be the one, at his side, called to manage what's been provided. Even if Kent and I had millions of dollars, I'd still shop at sales and establish a budget. There is much dignity and peace derived from handling your expenditures well! I'm not even married yet, and I love imagining the feeling of settling my head on my pillow after grocery shopping really wisely, seeing Kent's look of surprise and happiness at how well we're eating for so little money and my hands happily exhausted from the day's tasks! How honoring and challenging to work in a budget that never harms your husband and glorifies your household. There is honor in the challenge! Mom, please pray for me that I can be all those things to Kent. It's my heart's dearest wish. I worry so because lately, especially, I've really been slapped in the face with how selfish I am. I almost despair at this at times! Thanks too, just for listening—sorry so much came out! What a noble calling to be Kent's wife! Soon to be a Weber girl! My heart leaps at it! It's amazing how much meaning my life has, in serving him. I do feel made for him. Funny, how it all works, eh? Thanks for entrusting your eldest to me. Mom, I love you! I treasure you, and can't wait to see you!*

*Love, Carolyn*

I'm glad so much kept "coming out." I see much value here in "letting" Carolyn share her heart through me to you. It has always been important to me that there be no wasted experiences in my life. I've appreciated opportunities to learn and grow from the example of others, whether good or bad. Carolyn's letter provides a positive example of a woman's desire to be a helpmate suitable for her husband. If we all had her attitude, we could multiply God's glory through our example. We could train our daughters and raise up God-honoring helpmates. We could be flesh and blood patterns for others to follow, influencing future generations. As Psalm 102:18-22 says, "This will be written for the generation to come; / That a people yet to be created may praise the LORD. . . . to serve the LORD."

Examples of both positive and negative behavior are provided frequently for us in Scripture. First Corinthians 10:11 says this: "Now these things happened to them as an example, and they were written for our instruction." I pray that Carolyn's letter as a faithful servant would reveal to you how to have the heart of God. Loving our husband is an extension of our prior commitment to God and is a biblical concept we can follow.

So let's have an attitude check. Dr. Toni Grant says, "Getting married does not so much demand that a woman do something, but rather that she be in the right frame of mind for bonding with a man. This frame of mind can be characterized as a uniquely feminine attitude, a particular way of being a woman."[1] Dr. Grant discusses how today's woman must learn to integrate her identity as a person of accomplishment with her needs for love and feminine fulfillment. The right kind of attitude toward feminine fulfillment will only come when our loving sovereign God has free rein in our life. Getting next to the Savior gives us pure light, which reflects in our attitudes.

# From the Beginning

The Creator, the Lord God, allowed us to come into being as He "formed man of dust from the ground, and breathed into his nostrils the breath of life; and man became a living being" (Gen. 2:7). The setting was perfect . . . except that it was incomplete. In His infinite wisdom, God planned that man not be alone.

As Adam watched the animals pass by in twos to be named, he probably couldn't help but feel an incredible sense of incompleteness. Some element in his life was missing. He might have said, "Hey! What's the deal here, Lord?" Adam was designed for compatibility. The Designer of all time and space, "the LORD God said, 'It is not good for the man to be alone; I will make him a helper suitable for him'" (Gen. 2:18). The Author, who wrote the script for that perfect world and the owner's manual for how to live in perfect harmony, went to work again. All knowing and all wise, He designed what was best for each.

With the touch of the most magnificent artist, "the LORD God fashioned into a woman the rib which He had taken from the man, and brought her to the man. And the man said, 'This is now bone of my bones, / And flesh of my flesh; / She shall be called Woman, / Because she was taken out of Man'" (Gen. 2:22–23). God chose to present the carefully designed counterpart to Adam as his custom-made helpmate. Woman was designed as a complement to enhance and bring fulfillment to man. What pleasure! The perfect unselfish giving of this ultimate pair reflects the glory of the magnificent God of the universe. Seeing this helpmate suitable after imagining Adam's incomplete feeling causes us to celebrate God's majesty. God does want to give us good and perfect gifts.

# Incredibly Essential

We recently built a new house. Most every section was carefully planned. The four front pillars represent the four pillars of a man's heart and reflect Stu's life message and book. As friends visit, my husband explains that the pillar by the kitchen is load bearing. It represents the strength behind him—the true helpmate who is suitable. That pillar is essential because it holds up the weight of the house. Similarly, a good wife supports her husband. A wife represents half the pieces that are necessary to complete the whole puzzle of marriage. She's not just a good idea; she's essential and helps her husband and family avoid chaos.

During the holidays, a large puzzle draws our family members to pause and place pieces. As we work, we find two pieces that were meant to fit into each other. They complement one another; they were meant to go together. Each piece is different, but they all are designed to fit together to complete the picture. It is necessary that those two pieces hook up. None of the other pieces fuse into a perfect union in puzzle terms!

What a picture! This is God's design for the human race. The man and the woman are puzzle pieces, if you will, for each other. If the whole puzzle were divided into twosomes, each piece would need the other to be complete. In the same way in marriage, each partner needs the other for completion. Who but an omniscient, omnipotent God could have created such harmony in diversity?

# Thinking Dually

A good helpmate thinks dually. It's "thee and me," not just "I, me, and my." To achieve the oneness that women were designed for, we think and act as a partner. We are team players whose concern is for the good of the whole. We don't mind not getting our name in the paper every time our team plays. We just want our team to win. When my first two children were under three, my husband started seminary. It was our goal to get him through school in preparation for his life work. Although I would have liked to take a course or two and be out of the house more often, I chose to think dually and do what was best for our team at that season.

By definition and God's will, women are side-by-side companions, soul-boosters, and encouragers of one another. Two draft horses that are quite notable alone become ever so much more efficient and strong when they are yoked together. Geese fly farther and expend less energy when they fly together. Solos in music are great, but when two voices or instruments harmonize and synchronize, the beauty of the music broadens and soothes the soul. In *Being a Woman*, Toni Grant compares harmony in life's relationships to harmonizing in music. She speaks of surrendering one's own pursuit to harmonize better with the other. "It is what my mother always called having a sense of otherness,"[2] says Dr. Grant. Singing harmony or living harmony requires paying much attention to the other person.

# Accessibility

Picture yourself walking into a beautiful fifteen-room house. If every door were open, you could look into each room and enjoy all the furniture and fabrics. You wouldn't have to wonder what was behind the closed doors or in the drawers and cupboards. You could admire the rows of shiny knives, forks, and spoons in the silverware chest. But if the doors, closets, drawers, and cupboards were locked, you would not have access to the complete beauty of the house.

In life, we want the interior of our home, our person, to be accessible. We don't want to withhold any good thing. In our marital relationships we need to be transparent, which means our husbands can see what's going on inside us. We share our hopes and fears, our victories and struggles. We also need to be available or supportive of them. If we are not both honest (transparent) and supportive (available to help), our husbands will have little access to the beauty of our interior being. Honest participation in another's life generates accessibility to oft-hidden rooms of our heart.

We don't want to experience bad consequences because we exert too much effort trying to be self-sufficient. We also don't want to cripple our relational ties and set ourselves up for emotional deficiencies. Sometimes we have no idea this has been happening to us because it is a below-the-surface phenomenon.

After about twenty years of marriage, a friend of mine shared that she was being convicted of not being open enough with her husband. She realized that because of her difficult childhood, she usually shared openly with those who only saw her once or twice a year. Such friends were usually physically distant, and this woman unconsciously thought that if they hurt her, it would be less traumatic than if a physically accessible person such as her husband rejected her. This woman told her husband of her self-discovery and asked him to help her to be more transparent by waiting to ask about her day and her feelings when the house was quiet and the children were cared for.

# Giving of Yourself

When you think of supporting someone's cause, what comes to mind? Helpfulness? Encouragement? Martha-types think of doing things for others. Mary-types find ways to listen and comfort emotionally. We provide strength to others as we *give of ourselves* to reinforce their cause—whether lofty or mundane.

Those around us are able to withstand outside forces partly because we contribute time, energy, and our best efforts. We ignore our own needs for a time as we immerse ourselves in giving. We look for ways to build them up. We imagine what we might want if we were in their place, and we rush to provide it.

Being a helpmate suitable requires the same efforts. We give and we give. There is no room for arrogance. We talk to our husband like he's a valued part of our life. We choose not to challenge or belittle his every move so as to not destroy his spirit. Instead, we strive to enable him to feel tall and stand tall through every challenge, especially amidst hard times.

# The Desired Profile

The Scriptures are full of descriptions of helpmates. *Prudence, encouragement, optimism*, and *responsibility* are key concepts.

## Prudence

Proverbs 19:14 says, "A prudent wife is from the LORD." Prudence means to be capable of exercising sound judgment in practical matters. Oh, that we would not be so intelligent in some areas and of so little earthly good in practical matters. Prudence is rather graphically described in Proverbs 11:22: "As a ring of gold in a swine's snout, / So is a beautiful woman who lacks discretion."

Let's describe a prudent woman a bit more. She is cautious or discreet in conduct, circumspect, not rash. She manages carefully and with economy; avoids danger; is wary; and considers all related circumstances before acting, judging, or deciding. This woman keeps silent or preserves confidences when necessary.

It's easy for us to assume we are prudent. A friend who knows us well may be a better judge. Reviewing our past decisions and examining the consequences can also help us become aware of the need in our lives for this godly quality.

## Encouragement

We like it when someone says nice things to and about us. We like it even if we don't deserve it. Our mates need this kind of love, which some-times doesn't always flow naturally. Proverbs 31:12 says, "She does him good and not evil / All the days of her life." This passage makes no men-tion of whether the husband deserves it, so we can assume that earned hon-ors aren't necessary. We should encourage others whether they deserve it or not. That is God's kind of love. However, sometimes we get in the way. We concentrate on ourselves so strongly that we can't get past that hurdle to lift our fellow comrade.

We encourage others best when we have dealt honestly with our own problems first. Joyce Landorf Heatherley says, "Before we understand how to be affirmers, we have to face the reality of rejection and its lethal force in our own lives. We need to deal with our own brokenness in order to move out into the world as affirmers."[3] Joyce goes on to help us evaluate whether or not we are affirmers. A casual word or sentence can change or lift the countenance of the one spoken to. Do you spot "sparks of original-ity" in another that others don't see? Go ahead and mention it to that per-son. Maybe you see a glimpse of someone's potential or think they may have a certain spiritual gift. Tell them about the brilliance you see. By affirming this person's potential you help renew their self-worth. By valu-ing them you help them believe in their own value. You encourage them to stretch and dream beyond their self-imposed limits and capabilities.[4]

We change the world by building and affirming others. Joyce Landorf Heatherley encourages us to become cheerleaders rather than discouragers. She says to others, "Let me hug you with my words."[5]

When we pass out compliments, we show respect. We honor our mate by showing and speaking admiration. Playing up his strengths and dimin-ishing his weaknesses will cause him to want to reach for excellence. Our encouragement can help him bypass his former limitations. Demonstrating sacrificial love will motivate him to act at new levels of efficiency and power. As we continue to remind him of his strong suits he will live in that realm and be prepared to reflect back the strengths he sees in us. We set ourselves up to win through our choice of encouraging behavior.

## Optimism

"Whatever is true, whatever is honorable, whatever is right, whatever is pure, whatever is lovely, whatever is of good repute, if there is any excellence and if anything worthy of praise, let your mind dwell on these things" (Phil. 4:8). Furthermore, "practice these things; and the God of peace shall be with you" (v. 9). That sounds like helpful advice for a peace-seeking helpmate. Fill your mind with all the positive remembrances you can muster.

First Corinthians 13:5 states that love "does not take into account a wrong suffered." It takes discipline of the mind to choose not to focus on wrongs. But it's worth it. One optimistic woman can change the whole mood of her home. Spend time following the admonition in Proverbs 14:1, "The wise woman builds her house," as opposed to, "the foolish tears it down with her own hands."

## Responsibility

In the following chapters, the areas of *committing, submitting,* and *loving* will be addressed. We will look at our actions as they affect our relationships.

We "signed up" to be next to our man when we married him. Life has taken on a new view. Without losing our individuality, we left behind our independence. Even our will and our body are not our own; we have given ourselves up for the oneness of a marriage relationship. Over the years, my husband has officiated at hundreds of weddings. He often tells the couple: "In God's marital economy, one plus one equals one. That is not quantum physics, but it is relational dynamics." Through marriage we accept responsibility to be an integral part of our mate's life.

Proverbs 31:23 relays how a woman's husband is "known in the gates." "Did you marry your husband to help him GET TO HIS GATE in better fashion than he could have done by himself?" asks Jo Stone in *Give Him His Gate*.

> Does it MATTER to you as to whether or not your husband MAKES IT TO HIS GATE?—Be it the gate of a lawyer, a handyman, missionary, statesman, mechanic, printer, pastor, engineer, electrician—whatever. His life's goals, so vital to a man who is going somewhere, are realized and there he is—IN HIS GATE!—His GOAL-GATE! It is publicly acknowledged, no matter how small the public, that this man who has made it to his GATE is not a square peg in a round hole.[6]

You possess qualities to take average talent and help him go all the way to the top. It's an opportunity you have to further his cause.

# Facts to Remember

Let's look at some biblical facts. God created the man first. He was in charge. Order was important. Responsibility was evident. God planned it all. Eve was given to Adam. She was beautiful. Choice was presented to her, and she chose wrongly. She was deceived. And tough consequences will continue to affect all for generations to come. The Lord God said, "'And I will put enmity / Between you and the woman, / And between your seed and her seed; / He shall bruise you on the head, / And you shall bruise him on the heel.' / To the woman He said, / 'I will greatly multiply your pain in childbirth, in pain you shall bring forth children; / Yet your desire shall be for your husband, / And he shall rule over you'" (Gen. 3:15–16).

The husband and wife are designed to be interdependent. First Corinthians 11:11 says, "However, in the Lord, neither is woman independent of man, nor is man independent of woman." As Mart DeHaan says, "God made women as partners, not property. Men and women were made for mutual respect and love, not exploitation and control."[7]

The Proverbs 31 woman presents numerous glances into the life of the talented and industrious helpmate. She treasures the lives in her care. Her provision is extensive. She does not bail out. She stays. She manages. She increases wealth. She creates worth. She takes pieces and makes something out of nothing, using her time wisely. What a woman!

These same character qualities have a strong place in God's design for single women. We can all practice the principles of being a helpmate in whatever realm we live. The quality of our service to others is a reflection of our relationship to God.

# Evaluation/Admonition Time

Alice Gray tells women to ask themselves these questions when evaluating their lives: "What is it like being married to me?" and "What is it like hearing the things I say?"[8] The answers to these questions often indicate what attitudes and actions we are sending to our loved ones. Being a helpmate is no easy job. Many women give up, as the divorce statistics prove. Our support can make the men we marry, or our neglect can destroy them. We have the influence to lift our man into positions above his natural abilities or to strip him of the dignity and momentum he presently possesses.

Have you ever observed the woman who demands control? She must have her way, regardless, or everybody pays. The well-known saying often applies: "If Mama ain't happy, ain't nobody happy." When a woman's need to control dominates a home's atmosphere, she counters God's intentions. God wants a wife to use every opportunity to complete her man. When she feels weak or selfish, she utters the words of Scripture: "'My grace is sufficient for you, for power is perfected in weakness. . . . for when I am weak, then I am strong'" (2 Cor. 12:9–10).

Neither husbands nor wives are perfect. My important self-evaluation before God is this: Is my love for God motivating my responses to life as a helpmate who is suitable for my husband? Like the rumbling of the earth before a volcano explodes, a woman whose heart is unsettled can disturb those around her. It is essential that we each obey God so we can become free to give wholly of ourselves.

# A Helpmate's Calling

God calls us to be helpmates who are suitable for our husbands. We are not called to convince, convict, coerce, and control our mates (to relay Andy Stanley's four features in a dysfunctional life).[9] That means we are to live out each of those words—*help*, *mate*, and *suitable*, as shown on the chart at the end of this chapter. The one-word descriptions will help us better understand our job as designated by the Creator. He gave us our jobs for our ultimate good and pleasure.

Being a speaker is a little like being a helpmate. When I enter a room, I can either set my audience at ease or I can put them on edge. I love to see how I can be helpful to them. I study them in advance so I tread carefully and begin where they are. I try to dress appropriately to show I'm part of them. I address concerns I know they have. I compliment them on the positive things they are doing. Hopefully this prepares their hearts to receive what I have to say. I know that coming before every group means facing people with differences. We'll never all agree, but our time together is every bit as important as the results.

When we abide by biblical principles as we learn how to be godly women, we can develop oneness that enhances our time together. We may labor through difficult experiences, but the darker the night, the brighter the light at the end. Then we can sing, "My God knows the way through the wilderness, all I have to do is follow."

# Allowing God's Change-Agents to Work

I join Mary Farrar in encouraging women to consider the following admonition as they strive to be a God-honoring helpmate suitable. "Find some woman who is crazy about her husband and hang closely around her." As my husband has often taught, three change-agents are available to us from God for our edification. Whether it is the Word of God, the Spirit of God, or the people of God that stimulate us to change any off-balanced life trend, we will do ourselves favors by being open to all three agents. "Iron sharpens iron" (Prov. 27:17). The following story illustrates how the Spirit of God helped me change my attitude as a helpmate.

There have been plenty of seasons that I haven't felt the joy of being a helpmate. I remember one day when I was busy packing for our speaking trip the next day. Our topic was "Oneness in Marriage." Only I wasn't feeling very worthy of the topic. You see, Stu had been gone sixteen hours that day expending all his energy toward ministry. The days prior had been somewhat similar. Of course, there needs to be a balance, and there are seasons that require more give in one direction than another. But where was my attention being directed? Myself! I was stewing over how *he* needed to be meeting *my* needs. I had developed quite a case, you can be sure.

As I peddled away on my exercise bike rehearsing my disappointments, I worked myself up into a lather, in more ways than one. Fortunately, the Spirit of God brought His ways to my remembrance and all those points that I teach flooded my mind. I started thinking about what I could do right in response. I could take the focus off myself and dwell on what I could do to make life easier for my husband.

I could greet him with a warm smile and caring tone to show a concerned interest in his tiredness after helping others that day. I could offer to rub his shoulders or feet and ask him questions about his day and be genuinely interested. Or I could complain about the demands that filled my life. And I could do a little demanding myself about things I felt he should change. Then again, I could show sympathy for what he's gone through, how he's had to deal with some delicate situations with hurting people. Or I could "read him the riot act" on how he's not meeting my needs or showing he even cares. I might chide him for another decision he's made without me and berate him in disagreement.

The choices were obvious. I was feeling taken for granted. But the Spirit of God convinced me to choose wisely and let the love of God motivate how I would respond. When Stu walked in, he knew he hadn't been helpful to me. He knew that I wanted more attention from him than I was getting. Yet, this time, I was able to let go of those natural responses and let God replace them with godly choices. It was great! Stu didn't expect it, to be honest, and we both enjoyed the warm interaction that softened our hearts toward one another.

# The Result

Attitude, attitude, and attitude. That is what makes the difference. Our attitudes are determined by how we develop our thinking patterns. Then our chosen actions take over and determine the results. Regardless of what our husbands' choices are along the way, our lives as a helpmate suitable can reflect the light of God to a broken world. Proverbs 31:28–29 states, "Her children rise up and bless her; / Her husband also, and he praises her, saying: / 'Many daughters have done nobly, / But you excel them all.'"

❧

## A HELPMATE SUITABLE

**P**
**O**
**S**

**H**
**E**
**L**
**P**

| | |
|---|---|
| ASSIST | CONTRIBUTE |
| SERVE | SUSTAIN |
| EASE | ENCOURAGE |
| NURTURE | FACILITATE |
| SUPPORT | IMPROVE |
| GIVE | CARE |

**M**
**A**
**T**
**E**

| | |
|---|---|
| COMPLEMENT | RECEIVER |
| APPROPRIATE | COMRADE |
| ASSOCIATE | FRIEND |
| COMPANION | CONFIDENT |
| COUNTERPART | PARTNER |
| SUPPLEMENT | MATCH |

**I**
**T**
**I**

### SUITABLE

| | | |
|---|---|---|
| AGREE | CORRESPONDING | FITTING |
| ADAPT | PLEASE | ACCOMMODATE |
| CORRELATIVE | GOOD | PROPER |
| RIGHT | WORTHY | ELIGIBLE |

**V**
**E**

| | | | | |
|---|---|---|---|---|
| Wise | Enduring | Supportive | Obedient | Compassionate |
| Sweet | Diplomatic | Responsive | Graceful | Hospitable |
| Receptive | Discerning | Perceptive | Charming | Considerate |
| Empathetic | Polite | Sensitive | Available | Enthusiastic |

**N**

Antonyms: (opposite of) Help, Mate, and Suitable

**E**

HELP – To hinder, ensnare, worsen, reject, aggravate, weaken, downgrade, cheapen, demote, trap, tangle, and embroil.

**G**
**A**

MATE – Foe, rival, enemy, opponent, competitor, betrayer, one who is estranged, disengaged, or antagonistic.

**T**

SUITABLE – Unfit, irrelevant, unacceptable, unsuitable, displeasing, silly, smothering, vain, uncontrolled, sloppy, spiteful.

**I**
**V**
**E**

| | | |
|---|---|---|
| Defensive | Independent | Angry |
| Controlling Personality | Superiority Complex | Self-centered |
| Inaccessible | Unapproachable | Confused Forever |
| Manipulative | Jealous | Moody |
| Petty | Prudish | Naive |
| Weepy forever | Passive | Discontent |

© Linda Weber 1999

CHAPTER 6

# Commitment, Submission, and Rebellion

$\mathcal{T}$he word *commitment* means a pledge or binding of a promise to do something; a responsibility, a duty, dedication to a long-term course of action; handing over or setting apart to put to some purpose; entrusting, implying committal based on trust and confidence. That definition doesn't exactly sound like marriage today, does it? Many men and women don't understand the kind of work necessary to make a marriage last.

The bride and the groom usually utter the biblical principle of commitment in their vows: "In sickness and in health, until death do us part!"

After six months or a year, however, the bride or the groom finds it easy to say, "Oops, this isn't as much fun as I thought it would be. I think I'll go another way." What they say in their vows and what they live have become inconsistent.

# Christian Commitment Connection

The idea of commitment is really counterculture. The Christian's first commitment, including a love connection, is to the Lord. Whatever or whoever else we become committed to should flow out of that original loyalty. Deborah Newman says this:

> You need to see your marriage vows as a covenant with God and not with your husband. When you view marriage this way, you are less likely to sever your vows based on what your husband does. You are promising God you will love, honor, and cherish your husband whether he deserves it or not.
>
> One day we will all stand before the judgment seat. As we face God, He will remind us, "I gave you that husband to love. How did you do?" We need to recognize the immense ministry that we are given right in our own homes with our own husbands.[1]

Because I love God, I want to serve Him through commitment to my husband. My love for God motivates me to love Stu, whether I feel like it or not. I'm meeting responsibility and opportunity on a higher plane than where my feelings flow. That means I need to nurture my love for God. As I do, I become motivated to remain committed in marriage.

How I choose to honor the Lord individually will show in the level of commitment I display with my mate. It's easy to be committed when things are going well. When differences "blow our minds" and stretch us to the limits of our endurance, our commitment levels are tested. "Do I really have to live like this?" we ask. "Don't I deserve better?"

# Commitment under Trial

In being a partner to our husbands, it's natural to focus on his short-comings. When life is less than ideal, we can get in the habit of blaming him for our problems. (We're unfortunately born with the natural sin bent, and blame is as old as Eve.) In the process, we underestimate the need to stick to our personal responsibilities. The easy response is to allow selfishness to run free like a wild horse. Our sour attitudes and sharp tongue give us away. Our countenance even displays our desire to save self at all cost.

Ruth Myers takes us to the principles of Scripture in her book *31 Days of Praise* and presents the godly progression of thinking we should have when bombarded with undesirable situations. God's thinking, as expressed by Ruth, will always get our runaway life back under control.

> Even in troubled circumstances, or when God does not choose to work in spectacular ways, praise can help us view our situation through different lenses. It can help produce within us a restful, invigorating inner climate.
>
> And often this change of climate within us helps transform the atmosphere around us, for our new attitudes cause people to react differently to us. We begin to exert a creative and uplifting influence on them.
>
> So praise brings obvious victory, or it enables us to turn apparent defeats (whether dramatic trials or minor irritations) into victory from God's viewpoint. It tunes out the conflicting voices that shatter our faith and block our love; and it tunes us in to God's guidance, so that we can discern what actions to take, if any.[2]

What happens when we praise? Ruth tells us: "When we praise, we enthrone God in our lives and circumstances, and He manifests His presence in a special way."[3]

# Help from God

When I choose to praise and thank God, even though things aren't the way I might like them to be, I receive a blessing in return. God grants me power to remain committed. At the wedding I say a pledge and make a binding promise to give myself to my mate. I have chosen to dedicate myself to my husband for the long-term, not for as long as I feel like it. As I focus on Scripture and the blessings I have from God, I discover that my attitude changes.

The rehearsing of Scripture always brings clarity to our minds. "'Have you not read, that He who created them from the beginning MADE THEM MALE AND FEMALE, and said, "FOR THIS CAUSE A MAN SHALL LEAVE HIS FATHER AND MOTHER, AND SHALL CLEAVE TO HIS WIFE; AND THE TWO SHALL BECOME ONE FLESH"? Consequently they are no longer two, but one flesh. What therefore God has joined together, let no man separate'" (Matt. 19:4–6). That is commitment.

# Under God's Scrutiny

First Corinthians 7:39 tells us, "A wife is bound as long as her husband lives, but if her husband is dead, she is free to be married to whom she wishes, only in the Lord." Other Scriptures refer to Moses permitting divorce because of hardness of heart (but not God's real choice) when the other party is guilty of adultery. Although there may be an "out" for those whose partners have committed adultery, my own mother has chosen to stay single for over thirty-seven years after her fifteen-year marriage ended in divorce.

We will answer to God for our actions. Our husbands will answer to God for their actions. God will handle the rewards and the punishments, for He says, "'VENGEANCE IS MINE, I WILL REPAY. . . . THE LORD WILL JUDGE HIS PEOPLE.' It is a terrifying thing to fall into the hands of the living God" (Heb. 10:30–31).

# Commitment Requirements

Once we enter a marriage relationship, we take on commitment requirements. Our duty now is to turn from old patterns, to accept a new identity, to count the cost, to care and honor, and to persevere.

## Turn from Old Patterns

In a simple but profound way the Bible says, "No one can serve two masters; for either he will hate the one and love the other, or he will hold to one and despise the other. You cannot serve God and mammon" (Matt. 6:24). A pitcher must be emptied of its contents before we can fill it with another substance. One electrical plug must be pulled from an outlet before we can plug something in its place.

Why is it so hard to see that we must turn from old patterns of selfish focus in order to enjoy new ones? When we marry, we must stop our independent lifestyle and incorporate our spouse into our world. God wants us to be free to be dependent on one another. Culture urges us to become free by being independent.

The question is: Am I committed enough to turn from old patterns? Am I willing to give up my independence? Ruth Senter helps us understand this concept,

> According to Scripture, nothing is so Christlike as "giving up." Nothing so freeing as surrender. Nothing that leads to such eternal consequences for both men and women.
>
> It is what Jesus did. (See Phil. 2.)
> It is what He calls us to do.
> It is at the very heart of the Gospel.
> Give up your life so you can find it again.
> Lose it so you can keep it.
> Of all the people recorded in Scripture who gave up something, not one gave up and lost. They gave up and kept.[4]

Can you imagine what could happen in your marriage if you gave God your insecurities? Let's just name a few old patterns that could be dropped to allow for a better way: aloofness, childishness, distancing oneself/hiding, rationalizing, dominating, gossiping, manipulating. Giving up the old allows room for a fresh start.

## Accept a New Identity

Pretend you were the color yellow before you married. Your fiancé was the color blue. Then you came together as one and became a new color—

green. What an amazing new identity! When we learn to think of being this new color, we start incorporating things around us to fit into our new color scheme. We accept our identity of being one with each other. We not only think, *I am he and he is me,* but we order our daily tasks and lives around this oneness.

Taking our husband's name is one way we accept a new identity. Accepting his relatives as ours is another way. Each family has their own special holiday traditions, and becoming a new married "color" requires that we mesh his family's traditions with our old family practices to produce new traditions that will be memorable for our own small family.

Accepting a new identity might mean learning a new hobby or sport. Although I've always been a sports fan, especially through my husband's and sons' involvement in many sports, many women don't relate well to this.

Deb wasn't always a football fan, but her husband was. "Even before we married," Deb said, "I learned that Sunday afternoons were made for watching football on TV. I couldn't see the sense in one guy throwing some ball while the rest of the players piled on top of one another! But I sat with Ken and his family. Each week I tried to understand one new thing. I also learned not to ask too many questions that would distract them from the game. But with persistence and a focused effort, I learned. I've been converted! My husband became so proud of me for becoming obviously involved. When he happened to overhear me ask a friend what the score was of a game, he could feel me identifying with his interest. That identity is really assured when he finds me giving recaps of important plays or my prediction of who will win a game to anybody I talk to."

## Count the Cost

How many of us have taken on some project and then realized that we didn't have the tools, time, talent, or money to follow through? Suppose I buy a gallon can of spaghetti sauce and decide to heat it up for guests tonight. As I start pouring it into my two-quart saucepan, I realize there is more sauce than the pan can accommodate. But I'm hosting a large group, and I know I'll need every bit of food. I try to squeeze all the contents into the pan. Sauce overflows and spills onto the burner and the floor. Now I'm really in trouble because some of the sauce will have to be thrown away. The stove is soiled, the floor needs to be mopped, and I'm frantic. Worse yet, some of my guests will not get enough spaghetti sauce.

Likewise, we sometimes don't count the cost needed to fulfill our responsibility as a helpmate. Many women commit to a husband and children. We may also commit to employment as well as extended family, neighborhood, and church activities. Beyond this, we enjoy hobbies and various interests. Somehow, we think we can do it all. Intellectually, we know we have twenty-four hours in a day, but we try to do the impossible. Things start spilling out of our twenty-four-hour saucepan. We become frantic, and everything around us suffers.

Jo Stone helps us think about counting the cost of our commitment to our man. She is concerned about the woman who takes on more fields to cultivate than she can physically tend.

"Titus 2:5 says that a wife is to be 'good natured.' When we don't 'consider our field,' no matter how those fields are beckoning for attention, we will not 'expand prudently,' but will, in fact, use up all our energies before our husbands or anyone else under our roof, gets the best pieces for themselves—the pieces that rightfully belong to them."[5]

## Care and Honor

If each of us is committed to her husband, we'll treat him as we do our own flesh. Ephesians 5:29 says, "For no one ever hated his own flesh, but nourishes and cherishes it, just as Christ also does the church." Commitment doesn't just happen, does it?

Joyce Landorf Healtherley gives tips we can apply to our marriage. "Then Jesus gave His men the formula for being *the best man*. He said, 'Your care for others is the measure of your greatness.' Think of that! My care for someone else is the measure, the determining factor, the depth, the magnitude, and the very touchstone of *my greatness*."[6] Stop and ponder the depth of this formula.

When we care, we show honor. We maximize the good and minimize the hard things. Deanna McClary was forced to deal with her commitment level years ago when her husband, Clebe, lost an arm and an eye in Vietnam.

That day she first saw him so dismembered was dark. She loved Clebe. She wanted him back and determined to place her commitment level into the highest gear to do whatever was required to help him.

> I had discovered my mission in life. I was going to person-
> ally nurse Patrick Cleburn McClary III back to health. I
> would be whatever he needed me to be . . . for the rest of
> our lives, I would in many respects be indispensable to
> him. This was an awful price to pay to be needed, but I
> determined from the beginning that I would never hold it
> over his head, demean him with it, or use it against him. I
> would help maintain his dignity.[7]

## Persevere

Only you can decide whether your commitment is worth it. The storms of life are going to blow hard. Pressures will surround us. Our commitment to be a helpmate will need constant mental and spiritual renewal. It is indeed harder work than most feats we'll accomplish in other areas.

When Stu and I got married, one of the songs at our wedding was from the story of Ruth in the Scriptures: "'For where you go, I will go, and where you lodge, I will lodge. Your people shall be my people, and your God, my God'" (Ruth 1:16). Those words were Ruth's story of commitment, and I wanted them to be mine as well. Does all this mean it's been easy? Not really, because good things usually require much. In the process of it all, I have chosen to persevere (to persist, not to quit).

I stayed close to God, remembered my "godly serious vow" and fol-lowed the suggestions of Scripture. Proverbs 11:14 says, "Where there is no guidance, the people fall, / But in abundance of counselors there is victory." Another word of encouragement toward pursuing help is in Proverbs 19:20, "Listen to counsel and accept discipline, / That you may be wise the rest of your days."

Regardless of how we grew up, even where there have been ongoing disappointments and hardships, we have hope. Our hope is in the Lord. We can walk through tough circumstances and failures. Our perseverance reflects the glory of God as we choose to shine as that God-ordained help-mate. May God help us all through this challenging opportunity.

# Misunderstandings about Submission

One year my husband and I were asked to present a marriage conference for a large ministry. Before we left home, a leader from the group called and asked that I avoid teaching on the subject of submission. A previous speaker had discouraged their audience and nearly lost their financial backing. As I contemplated this, I knew it would not be possible to fulfill the request. To teach God's idea of marriage without mentioning submission was impossible. I called and told them that I must include this important teaching. If it is God's ordained way, then we must understand and implement it to enjoy life abundantly. They agreed.

Submission is an easy concept to misunderstand and an easy concept to misuse. Some young women in our church have asked my husband not to use the "S word" in their wedding ceremonies. Yet when they came to a right understanding of submission, they realized that it is a necessary piece in the beautiful puzzle of marriage. Biblical submission reflects a commitment to God first, which in turn manifests itself as a pattern of Christlike responses to our husbands. This concept is defined more fully in the chart on page 82. Our perspective can become skewed so easily.

Do you remember June 1998 and the shock with which news organizations reported the Southern Baptists' statement of belief that wives should submit? Judging by the reaction to the Baptists' statement, you would think that this principle was some new threat to be protected from. Instead, the word that strikes fear in the public mind because of a false concept is the word God chose to use to ensure protection for the feminine creature He so skillfully designed. It is wonderful when women come to appreciate the Creator's definition and see that we reflect His image as we follow Christ's example. Let's allow Him to paint the picture of His intended meaning behind His definition.

# Help Me See My Model

Understanding God's intention requires going back to the basics. A study of Christ's life enables us to possess a model of submission to emulate. As we read through key passages of His life (see Eph. 5:25–27 and 1 Pet. 2:21–24), we find behaviors we must practice.

When our goal is to please God by being obedient to Him, we will love others the way He loves, and His love will overflow. God's love is like a lump of dough that rises and rises and pours over the edge of the pan. When we take on His kind of love—the way He loved through submitting to the Father's will—we become enabled to submit as Jesus did. Jesus is our model for submission. Submission is a natural outgrowth of our love for God. As we submit to our husbands, God's kind of love overflows through us and extends out to others.

To be submissive is to walk in Him and love our husbands unconditionally. Our unselfishness and care become a choice. Colossians 2:6–7 helps us see our need to choose God's way: "As you therefore have received Christ Jesus the Lord, so walk in Him, having been firmly rooted and now being built up in Him and established in your faith, just as you were instructed, and overflowing with gratitude." So our good attitude can show gratitude through submission to our husbands. We love because He first loved us. We choose submission because of the God factor in our life; we want to bring honor and glory to the God who loves us so.

# Important Facts about Submission

Godly submission requires deliberate action, an understanding that order is essential for a strong marriage, and knowledge that God's ways are best.

## It Requires Deliberate Action (the Extra-Mile Type)

Susan Hunt says this: "Submission is not about logic; it is about love. Jesus loved us so much that He voluntarily submitted to death on a cross. His command is that wives are to submit to their husbands. It is a gift that we voluntarily give to the man we have vowed to love in obedience to the Savior we love."[8]

Jesus also said it this way: "'Unless a grain of wheat falls into the earth and dies, it remains by itself alone; but if it dies, it bears much fruit. . . . if anyone serves Me, the Father will honor him'" (John 12:24, 26). The way up is down—the essence of submission.

Robert Lewis and William Hendricks help us understand where the real action surfaces—our responses.

> Submission is not the woman's role in marriage. For years I thought it was. Like most of us, I was taught that the role of the husband was to be the leader and the role of the wife was to submit. The husband was to be assertive, active, aggressive, and creative. The wife was to be more or less compliant, passively going along with her husband's direction. Over time I began to see what a tremendous error that was. . . . So where does that leave submission? I believe submission is not a role at all, in the technical sense. A better definition would be to describe it more as a response than a role.[9]

What good reminders! Our Christlike responses are the kinds of actions that will affirm and motivate our husbands to fulfill their role as servant leaders.

## Order Is Essential

Compare a strong corporation to a strong marriage. The corporation's president makes decisions and leads his group into progressive action, which is a similar picture in marriage. If the president didn't have vice presidents providing critical information, it would be difficult for him to make wise decisions; his effectiveness would be diminished. With his team, the company is less likely to experience failure.

While Stu was in the army, we spent four-and-a-half years living all over the world. We observed how orderly the army was and that without order, chaos would rule. Everybody had a rank and answered to somebody. Could you imagine hundreds of thousands of people going to war without rank or order? Everyone would do what he or she thought best without regard to others. Organization happens where each person follows literal orders from his or her superior. Respect and obedience are crucial for maintaining that order.

In a marriage, there are many daily decisions. Two different opinions will surface regularly, so we need to interact intelligently and compassionately with our spouse to come up with a plan. Each of our gifts and strengths will surface in different places. Your insight into his gifting will help set him up to be the leader God intended. Placing yourself under that umbrella of headship will relieve pressure God never intended you to bear.

When Stu and I were newlyweds, I remember a big decision was made that I could not understand. While Stu was finishing Wheaton College, the plan was to go to seminary first and fulfill his four-year army obligation afterward. We were accepted as students at Gordon College and Seminary in Massachusetts, having been appointed to specific jobs as well. We even moved our belongings to Boston during spring break before the start of the fall term.

In April, Stu decided we would pursue the direction of the army first. We were far into our plans, and at the time I was bewildered, to say the least. Years later, I realized how important it was for him not to have gone to seminary then. His heart wasn't ready, and he wouldn't have profited from the time. Our lives took a different route for our ultimate good, although at the time the change required my support and hard work. God had plans that I couldn't see. Whether or not we like it or understand it, God works through order. Trusting God enables us to follow the lead of the husband we chose to marry. He gives us many opportunities to put this principle to the test!

## Submission Is God's Way

The husband will rule over the wife, says Genesis 3:16, and she is expected to "be submissive to [her] own husband . . ." (1 Pet. 3:1). Ephesians 5:22, Colossians 3:18, and Titus 2:5 detail the same responsibility of submission. It is

God's way, and God's ways are for our good (Deut. 5:29). The best way we can take care of ourselves is to place our lives in God's hands. It's our privilege to submit and God's job to relieve pressure and resolve life's issues. Susan Hunt says it this way: "She does not have to grasp; she does not have to control. Her fear dissolves in the light of God's covenant promise to be her God and to live within her. Submission is simply a demonstration of her confidence in the sovereign power of the Lord God. Submission is a reflection of her redemption."[10]

# Is Your God Big Enough?

The more we get to know God, the more comfortable we are in submitting, in trusting God, and in letting our husband lead and/or make mistakes. Does your God know enough to take you through your present wilderness? Can He handle your husband or your circumstances? Is He powerful enough to make things happen? It certainly takes the burden off our shoulders when we acknowledge that "my hope is in Thee" (Ps. 39:7) and not my husband.

Knowing a big God also prevents us from responding, "But, but, but." The title of the booklet *But You Don't Know Harry*[11] won't be our response when we let our big God lead us in biblical submission.

A life verse for me is "'With men this is impossible, but with God all things are possible'" (Matt. 19:26). Whether it is submission or another challenge, we will reflect God's light as we let Him love through us.

# Men Have Heavy Duty

We are not the only ones given dutiful instruction on how to live the God-ordained life. Ephesians 5:21 tells *all* that we are to "be subject to one another in the fear of Christ." After addressing the women, Paul then gives the husbands a descriptive view of how they are to love their wives.

Husbands are not exempt from hard work; indeed they are required of God to love their wives "as Christ also loved the church and gave Himself up for her" (Eph. 5:25). He goes on to tell why and how. They must love their wives as they would care for their own bodies. Verses 29 and 30 are clear: "For no one ever hated his own flesh, but nourishes and cherishes it, just as Christ also does the church, because we are members of His body."

The biblical concept of submission includes a job of the husband. He is to live out those definitions—to give himself up sacrificially in service. He has obligations to adapt to living with his woman "in an understanding way, as with a weaker vessel, . . . and grant her honor as a fellow heir of the grace of life, so that your prayers may not be hindered" (1 Pet. 3:7). Christ's example puts heavier responsibility on the man than many realize. And should he fail to fulfill his duty, he will pay a price, and his prayers will be hindered.

# Rebellion

There are reasons women have difficulty submitting to their husbands. These same reasons are responsible for much confusion. Let's identify the problems: (1) That old sin nature from birth shouts, "I'll do what I want to do." (2) Many see submission as a negative, so they avoid it. (3) God is seen as smaller than her tough circumstances. (4) The definition has been maligned. Naturally, women oppose that which has become degradation. (5) Sinful behavior brings frustration and a lack of direction in dealing rightfully with submission.

Christine McClelland expresses her confusion regarding responsibility to submission this way:

> I never thought I would support that ugly "S" word. I wish I could change the world's definition of it. But at least I changed mine. [Before this happened, she had said,] Listening to my husband and doing what he says are two different things, based on my definition of submission: yielding when it is convenient. None of that Ephesians 5:22 wimpiness for me! I can take care of myself quite well, thank you. I certainly don't need a man to tell me what to do, considering the stupid mistakes men make. Marriage is a 50-50 deal: Both have input. When we don't agree, we argue until I win. It's that simple.[12]

Chris did change her definition and her attitude. "Women who stand against today's liberal dogma will glorify God with their submissiveness. Their humility will make an impression on disobedient husbands and win them "without a word" (1 Pet. 3:1–4).[13]

# Response to Rebellion

We definitely need to know what biblical submission does and does not look like. The purpose of the chart on page 82 is to set forth a clearer picture of biblical submission. You may be able to see why many have rebelled so strongly. Many face their own self-orientation, and of course that brings rebellion when it's challenged.

Some have felt forced into a certain pattern of living, which is not God's desire for submission. I hope you will take a lifetime to think about and act upon this truth. Is there ever an occasion not to submit? Tough questions have complex answers. We need always to submit to our highest calling—the instruction and example of Christ. Portraying the gracious side of Christ's example—giving, serving, and sacrificing—is God's intention.

Yet this same God hates sin and expects us to implement His kind of responses to wrongful patterns. One must have sound wisdom from the Father's heart to know how to make His choices. We will need to develop much skill, and that comes as we immerse our hearts and minds in Scripture and as we use the submission muscle to obey God. Only then will we know when and how to evaluate our situations and make the best response. Being submissive to God in response to sinful patterns demonstrates a side of submission that we sometimes disregard. See the chart for some guidelines regarding multiple aspects of submission.

When we don't understand, Deuteronomy 29:29 can give us guidance: "The secret things belong to the LORD our God, but the things revealed belong to us and to our sons forever, that we may observe all the words of this law." Christlike responses to sin are revealed, and yet there are no easy answers.

# To Submit or Not to Submit?

When faced with a sin of our husband's, do we submit or not submit? We are obligated to apply every biblical principle, not just those that are easy to do or readily understandable. Marriage is intended to last until death do us part. We bear responsibility for furthering the reputation and image of God through our actions. Commitment means to love our mate in all seasons, in sickness and in health, during the good, the bad, and the ugly. When considering tough choices, we must know the fear of God because we are accountable to Him. Submission to God and our husband is a godly principle.

We're born as sinners. So then, what level of sin is necessary to invoke our refusal to enable or endorse our husband's sin? Jesus provides biblical principles to follow and not pat answers. We know God expects us to be responsible in the area of accountability for our sins. We also know we are to live in submission to our husbands. Where the two might seem to overlap, we need God's scales to weigh all His expectations and to translate those expectations into a clear sign of advice. Therefore, I won't be drawing a line here; God desires to do that with you. Black and white answers are dangerous.

# Incredible Evaluation Is Necessary

We've looked at some reasons submission is difficult for women. There may be other influences. Perhaps the following questions could help sort out some issues. Could the frustration be rooted in the man-woman differences? (This is enough to frequently disorient us.) Are the issues of concern a matter of personal preference or opinion? Is your forbearing spirit observable with plenty of forgiveness during his selfish and sinful moments? Maybe there is a mental illness. Is it clear whether issues are real or possibly perceived? There are many factors to consider, and God's reputation is at stake.

We know our husbands do answer to God for their behavior. In the process of living next to our man, it's a difficult task to go against the grain and not encourage him. We want to enable and encourage positive patterns. The question is: How do I most responsibly submit to Christ's example (of submission) in my present situation? These kinds of issues are delicate and require extensive consideration. When he might break the law the answer is most obvious. It's about those other times when he's rather selfish and generally not living out God's kind of profile that have us baffled. Encouraging behavioral changes needs guidance from the wisest Christian counseling.

There are simply no easy answers in deciding how far is too far to go in "tolerating" his folly because the issue is complex. We know God allowed tyrants in the Bible to go through a growing process in becoming people after God's heart. Peter says we can even win our husbands without a word. Our silence, being prayerful and highly obedient to our responsibilities with a sweet spirit, can be used of God to move mountains. We need much patience, kindness, and self-control. We must extend incredible grace, as God would. We are usually emotionally involved, which means we especially need biblical counsel when sorting out precariously tough choices. In the process, a renewal of utmost respect for our vow in marriage is essential.

# God Says "No" to Extremes

The following incident is shared not for its sensational effect but as a warning within this discussion of submission. A woman we knew lived out this horrific story, and it was wrong.

This woman stood by as her husband beat their little boy for hours, in the name of breaking the will of the child. Even after the child died that evening from the destructive treatment, she supported her husband's actions, feeling this was submission. Of course, the husband went to jail for manslaughter. But because this woman supported her husband's sinful actions, the state removed their daughter from her home. Although most would never come close to this drastic trauma, submission to a sinful husband has a limit. There are laws against abusive behavior, and we want to remember other Scriptures, such as submit to governing authorities (1 Pet. 2:13) and do not murder (Exod. 20:13), that apply to this situation.

# Continually Rehearse Scripture

Many other cases present a gray line. Whatever your husband's issues might be, you are called to demonstrate Christlike responses. Studying 1 Peter 2:13–25, we become familiar with God's plan of honoring authority. This passage speaks of finding favor with God as we do what is right, even as we suffer for it and patiently endure trouble (v. 20). We become familiar with Christ's incredible example in verses 21–25 (see the left side of chart, page 82). Peter continues to address wives in 1 Peter 3:1–6:

> In the same way, you wives, be submissive to your own husbands so that even if any of them are disobedient to the word, they may be won without a word by the behavior of their wives, as they observe your chaste and respectful behavior. And let not your adornment be merely external—braiding the hair, and wearing gold jewelry, or putting on dresses; but let it be the hidden person of the heart, with the imperishable quality of a gentle and quiet spirit, which is precious in the sight of God. For in this way in former times the holy women also, who hoped in God, used to adorn themselves, being submissive to their own husbands. Thus Sarah obeyed Abraham, calling him lord, and you have become her children if you do what is right without being frightened by any fear.

Dr. Earl Radmacher told me how various wives have shared their tragic stories with him over the years. In each case, he counseled the wife to go home and memorize the above passage. After repeating this out loud many times daily and practicing its truth for several months, each woman was encouraged to return to talk further. In most every case, the women saw "miraculous" changes in their previously defiant husbands. This is good advice for all of us.

# Two Sides of the Same Coin

Humbly submitting to God and then, in turn, to our husband is the Master's design for true fulfillment as we initiate the gracious behavior of unselfishness. A Colossians 2 passage illustrates how there can be two sides to a same issue, like a coin that has two sides. In verses 6 and 7 we are told, "As you therefore have received Christ Jesus the Lord, so walk in Him, having been firmly rooted and now being built up in Him and established in your faith, just as you were instructed, and overflowing with gratitude." That's the positive expectation to pursue.

Then comes the cautious warning of how to proceed most circumspectly, so as not to get into trouble. "See to it that no one takes you captive through philosophy and empty deception, according to the tradition of men, according to the elementary principles of the world, rather than according to Christ" (2:8). Then, verses 16 and 18 proceed to further warn, "Let no one act," and "let no one keep defrauding you."

If your husband imposes destructive sinful demands on you, your submission to God can possibly require that you take specific action against the sin. (Again, learning how to identify destructive sin before God with *only* His definition is necessary.)

You may need to take a stand against obviously sinful patterns of consequence, since God never desires us to choose to participate in sin. Instead, strong action must take place to honor God's ways, rather than allowing compromise to invoke sinful action of our own.

Procuring strong biblical counsel is necessary to help protect us from any unwise choices we might lean to in our confused state. Advice is only as good as the advisor, so choose with much care.

# Sin Must Stop

In Acts 5:1–11 we read of the story of Ananias and his wife, Sapphira. When he sold a piece of property, he kept some of the money for himself. The rest he laid at the apostles' feet, telling them his donation was the full selling price. Peter confronted him about his lie, and Ananias literally dropped dead. His wife acted in full submission ("with his wife's full knowledge") to her husband's folly. She even proceeded to lie further. Guess what? She dropped dead as well. Peter had been compelled to ask her, "Why is it that you have agreed together to put the Spirit of the Lord to the test?" (v. 9). There's a principle for us to heed here.

Our sin nature nudges our husbands and ourselves to be selfishly oriented. Perhaps Sapphira could not have prevented her husband from lying, but she could have told the truth regardless. And sometimes if we speak up, God can use our standards to influence others.

Sue worked as the office manager/secretary in a tiny sales company. One morning her boss received a phone call from a man he did not want to speak to. Sue's boss instructed her to lie, saying, "Tell him I'm not in."

"I'm not good at lying," Sue responded, "because I think it's wrong. May I just say that you're not available?"

Sue's boss reluctantly agreed. "But when he calls back, say, 'I just stepped out.'"

"If you want me to say you just stepped out," Sue said, "then you better actually step out. Don't tell me where you go. Just go." Throughout the day when this particular person called, Sue's boss would run down the hall or out of the building and Sue would say, "He was here a minute ago. He just stepped out."

By 3:00 P.M. the caller caught on and asked Sue if she knew why her boss did not want to speak to him. "You'll have to answer that," Sue said. "But if I knew I'd tell you."

"I believe you would," the caller said. "Tell _____ he can stay in his office. I won't call anymore."

Sue's heart pounded as she relayed the message to her boss. A look of disbelief and relief flooded his face. "I guess making me step out was a good idea after all."

We cannot change those around us, whether it's about lying or exaggerated sin, but we must take seriously our own responsibility before God. Whenever we take a stand, we must first examine our motives. "'First take the log out of your own eye, and then you will see clearly to take the speck out of your brother's eye'" (Matt. 7:5). In the housecleaning of my life, I need to get rid of my own debris first. Then, I will be ready to support and honor my mate with his spring-cleaning.

We are to submit and give grace. But when there is a cancerous sin destroying the heart and spirit of a marriage, a family, or our close surroundings, it must be dealt with. The woman looks to God for ways to confront, reprove, and restore. She must not encourage sin's development but carefully follow God's principles in dealing with the sin.

# Choosing to Reflect Light

Few of us like conflict, but being submissive to God means pursuing a godly life through obedience. Besides portraying the gentle, meek, and mild side of Jesus, we are to hate sin and not to allow its patterns to rule us.

This concept of submission is indeed weighty. It carries with it great opportunity to reflect light directly from the heart of God. As women truly grasp the breadth of it all, and respond properly, we become mirrors of light. Then our beauty shines out to a world that is crying for this picture of completion.

As we've been standing, so to speak, in front of the mirror, what have we seen? Like the surprise piece of spinach I found in my teeth after being at an elite tennis club, maybe you have become aware of some unsubmissive responses in your life. God will illumine darkened corners.

Mary, the mother of Jesus, showed such maturity and wisdom as she responded in submission to all that God chose to do through her. She "treasured up all these things, pondering them in her heart" (Luke 2:19). She was richly rewarded and cared for by God! If we found ourselves in Mary's place, what would our response be?

Whether it's submission or any other directive we find in Scripture, we always need to start with acknowledging who God is. God is all knowing. Nothing takes Him by surprise. He is sovereign—in control of all things. He has all power to take us through whatever we face, and He always keeps His promises.

God can allow circumstances to remind us to come to Him as our refuge. What will save us is doing as God would have us do. We can follow the example of godly women mentioned in 1 Peter 4:19 who entrusted "their souls to a faithful Creator in doing what is right." May our attitudes of submission be like Christ's as we own our personal responses.

❦

## BIBLICAL SUBMISSION
## IS A RESPONSE
## TO CHRIST'S EXAMPLE

- Acknowledge headship
- Place self under authority
- Accept
- Support/be loyal
- Serve/encourage
- Sacrifice
- Give and give more, unconditionally
- Choose unselfishness
- Extend much grace
- Show allegiance/obedience
- Acknowledge other's importance (Phil. 2)
- Expect no rights
- Forgive/return no evil
- Please God the Father
- Complete your man
- Utter no threats
- Offer no deceit
- Offer no reviling/love enemies
- Speak and do no evil

**Which makes you:**

Responsive
Obedient/faithful
Adaptable
Flexible
Agreeable

### (While Exercising the Following)

- ✓ Prayer
- ✓ Discernment
- ✓ Faithfulness
- ✓ Self-control
- ✓ Patience
- ✓ Kindness

Action Necessary

- Determine & activate personal responsibility FIRST

- Learn to know what sin is and how to call sin a sin

- Realize the damage sin brings

- Let Scripture give steps to take

- Recognize sinful patterns/reroute your responses (no denials)

- Reject participation with sin/choose God's way (no enabling or codependency)

- Intervene/be proactive against sin (no minimizing)

- Disrupt destructive patterns/break sin's grasp (change status quo)

- Confront/reprove (speak truth in love)

- Enact restoration plans/try new avenue (seek wise counsel)

---

Biblical Submission is NOT

| | |
|---|---|
| Obedience to sin | Encouraging foolish acts |
| Refusing God's way | Being indifferent or passive |
| Avoiding conflict | Contradicting biblical principles |
| Breaking the law | Powerlessness |
| Viewing women as inferior | Doing wrong |
| Remaining aloof from God's Word | Remaining silent about sinful patterns |
| Being battered/threatened | Being trampled |

---

## TAKE A LIFETIME TO THINK AND ACT ON THIS

## CHAPTER 7

# Building Your Marriage

$\mathcal{A}$ happy marriage doesn't just happen. It takes a lot of work. I know that from experience.

As the eldest child in each of our families, my husband and I are both strong-willed, and we've had to work at overcoming this in our marriage. We didn't automatically know how to have a strong marriage; we've had to learn. We've sought to know God's plan as we've prayed daily and talked with wise counselors. Proverbs 11:14 says, "For lack of guidance a nation falls, but many advisers make victory sure" (NIV). I pray that you are open to the guidance of wise counsel.

Christian marriages today are going downstream in a fast-moving current. We're about to drift over the edge of the falls, and we don't even know it. We have become numb to the destructive currents surrounding us. We can't allow ourselves to be swept away. If couples are going to learn to swim against the tide, there's a lot of work to be done. This chapter is designed to give some hands-on help on how you can aid your husband in building a strong marriage. When you encourage your man so that he feels your desire for oneness, your marriage will be stronger and the motivation for developing a strong family will be strengthened as well.

As a wife, you are the key to motivating your husband in these areas. I was reminded of this recently when, after working at home all day, I received a call from Stu. He, too, had been working all day and had been in several intense meetings. He'd called at the end of his sessions to see how I was, as he knew I was under pressure. He asked if I would mind if he made a quick stop on the way home to check on his parents (now in their seventies). Even though I was tired and wanted to unload my frustrations, I encouraged him to check on his parents and said I was looking forward to seeing him when he got home.

Later that evening he thanked me for my upbeat attitude and for supporting his choice to visit his parents. He told me that when he'd called, he was exhausted and was unsure of how my demanding day would have affected me. When he detected in my voice that home would be an inviting safe place, he greatly anticipated coming home.

I'm glad I made that choice that evening. I don't always. I saw once again how great my influence is in motivating and energizing my husband. You have the same influence in your marriage. How can *you* support and encourage your husband to build a strong marriage?

# Know Your Man

Before you can support and encourage your husband, you need to know him. You need to know what tickles him, what makes him tick, and what ticks him off.

Learn about his masculinity. When a man is encouraged to be the man he was intended to be, everybody wins. He soars with confidence, his wife's needs are fulfilled, and his children's hopes are realized. In *Tender Warrior*, my husband says that God's intention for a man is that he always be an initiator, but never a tyrant . . . always a provider and protector, but never a brute . . . always a mentor and model, but never a know-it-all . . . always a friend and lover, but never a smotherer.[1]

As we support God's plan rather than try to force our husbands into our mold, they truly become what we are longing to have. We do ourselves a big favor when we become students of the differences between men and women.

Encourage your husband to pursue relationships or activities that develop his masculinity. For example, men need strong friendships with other men. In his book *All the King's Men*, Stu talks about how he suspects that David's relationship with Bathsheba would never have flourished if David had had an accountable relationship with Jonathan at the time.[2] According to my husband, men need other men to encourage their growth and to keep them accountable. As wives, we would be wise to invite such friendships rather than resent the time our husbands spend away from us.

If your husband has a friendship with someone who is a negative influence in his life, you should tactfully speak up about his choice of friends. Instead of condemning his actions and thereby raising his defenses, ask him questions about his friends. When you precede these talks with prayer, God will help you discern what questions will reveal these men's character and in turn show your husband what kind of behavior the relationships are producing. As he hears himself talk, he may realize that his behavior is destructive both to himself and to your relationship.

Give your husband the freedom to pursue recreation with other men. Whatever his passion—hunting, fishing, golf, carpentry, cycling—let him enjoy it in the company of other guys. Stu and I have three sons, so I'm the only female in our house. I've had to remind myself that they need time together without me so they can enjoy activities that have more masculine appeal. It takes conscious awareness on my part not to have a pity party.

# Enhance Your Sex Life

One of the best ways to a man's heart is through meeting his sexual needs. Whether you meet him at the door in Saran wrap (remember *The Total Woman?*) or find your own ways to be creatively tantalizing, expend some energy to meet the sexual needs God has instilled in him. Sex is usually a much more powerful force in our husband's lives than in ours. Don't minimize its importance.

The Bible clearly states that we are to enjoy sex with our spouse. Proverbs 5 advises men to avoid the seductions of an adulteress whose speech is smoother than oil (v. 3), and instead, "Drink water from your own cistern, / running water from your own well. . . . Let them be yours alone, / never to be shared with strangers. May your fountain be blessed, / and may you rejoice in the wife of your youth. . . . may her breasts satisfy you always, / may you ever be captivated by her love" (vv. 15, 17–19, NIV).

Wives can heed this admonition by relaxing. The entire Song of Songs describes the pleasures of a physical relationship between a man and a woman. Are we listening? Where did some Christians ever get the idea that sex was intended for procreation only? Our husbands are waiting for us, and they need our sexual attention—frequently. God made them that way, and He designed our incredible differences to blend together and complement one another.

As you increase your awareness of the differences between men and women, you will be able to pursue your husband with greater skill. Learn to enjoy him thoroughly. Let your body satisfy him. If we continually point out our body's faults, we disrupt his enjoyment. Focus on giving pleasure. Think about pleasing him. Vary positions and place. One of the best ways to keep your husband from being tempted to go elsewhere is to keep the chemistry burning between you. Keep him satisfied, and no other woman will be a serious temptation.

Since men are visual, we can support our husbands by paying attention to what they see when they look at us. Yes, we could respond to this by arguing, "What about him and his responsibilities? It's what's on the inside that matters anyway." While this is true, it's also true that taking active responsibility can be right before God. I've found that I'm much more effective if I concentrate on what I can do rather than focusing on my disappointments or another person's responsibilities.

Ask yourself, *What have I done to keep fit and be attractive? Do I care how I ring his bell and bring him running, even years after I won his heart?* Consider whether exercise should be a part of your formula. It helps to decrease lethargy and can increase your ability to be tuned into and alive for your husband.

During lovemaking, does your mind ever start wandering? Do you think, *Oh, shoot, I forgot to make the Jell-O, and now my dish won't be ready in time for company. . . . I wonder what I should fix for dinner tomorrow when our friends come over. . . . I wonder if the kids can hear this bed squeaking. Is the door locked? Are the plants watered? Curtains closed? Did I lay out the package I need to mail tomorrow?* You will be a better lover if you learn to discipline your mind when making love with your husband. Because it's natural for a woman's antennas to be up at all times, we're aware of what's happening or what needs to happen. Unfortunately, this means that during lovemaking our thoughts can be elsewhere if we do not discipline our minds. If we're not mentally present, our husbands will know it and get a message that we aren't interested.

As wives, we need to be aware that we have this tendency to split our attention among many things. Then we need to work hard to concentrate on our husbands and what we can do to be all we can be for that moment.

# Have Fun Together

You will enjoy your marriage more if you laugh a lot together. Try to find ways to experience pleasure that endears you to each other. Enjoy fun little names for each other that mean something special just to the two of you. Develop secrets together, private jokes that keep you whispering fun nothings and keep you intrigued with each other. Wink at him, and watch him melt. He'll love it.

Schedule time to go out and do something fun, even if your budget is tight. Be creative. Find ways to make fun happen. Instead of thinking, *Oh, we can't do that!* find a way; be persistent and watch your dreams come true.

My friend Lisa has learned how to do this on a shoestring budget. She read Mike Yorkey's book *Saving Money Any Way You Can,*[3] which offered lots of ways to save money on a daily basis, even on necessities like groceries, housing, and cars. The money she saved on these things allowed her to set aside some of their budget for fun times. Lisa realized that living on a tight budget could cause stress in a marriage, so she wisely made sure that she and her husband didn't sacrifice spontaneity and fun.

Another way to have fun is to make memories together. Find enjoyable things to do, and then record them in photos. Display these photos in frames around your home or office. The reminders of your special times together help endear you to each other and stimulate you to make more memories.

As you plan, think *togetherness* rather than independence. Plan events you can anticipate together. Show interest in his world and what he does and enjoys. During a recent sabbatical Stu went on a trip to his birthplace, which he had not seen in many years. He needed a little time away to enjoy reflecting on a lot of things that are important to him. That may not sound like entering his world, but because I was happy for him to have this time away, he knew that I cared about what was important to him. In his frequent calls home, he was bubbling to share with me the fun of seeing this or doing that or just remembering good times. I loved getting excited with him, and I was glad that he wanted to share his feelings with me. It was my privilege to enter his world by being interested and happy for him. It was good for us.

# Love Him Unconditionally

Loving your husband unconditionally means loving him even if he doesn't change or perform as you'd like. This is God's way of loving. Does it come naturally to any of us? No. We are born self-centered. We think, *What about me and what I want?*

When I speak with other women about this, I typically hear, "But you don't know my husband!" Loving unconditionally means loving someone despite his behavior. How many times have you refused to accept your husband because he hasn't lived up to your expectations? Maybe he doesn't fix things around the house that have been broken for months, even years. Maybe he stays at work and doesn't participate in household duties. He might forget things that are important to you. Or perhaps he spends money foolishly or has his priorities out of order. (Are they truly out of order or just not in your order?)

As Christian women, you and I can choose to put others first and accept the responsibility of doing what's right. Or we can choose to accuse and condemn our husbands. Being unselfish means loving with acceptance, regardless of performance. Does your husband feel in his bones that you love him as he is, or does he sense that you're waiting for him to change before you cherish him unconditionally?

# Be Supportive

Does your spirit motivate your husband to be a leader in your marriage? John Piper helps us understand God's intention for male-female relationships in his booklet *What's the Difference?* He says, "The biblical reality of a wife's submission would take different forms depending on the quality of a husband's leadership. This can be seen best if we define submission not in terms of specific behaviors, but as a *disposition* to yield to the husband's authority and an inclination to his leadership."[4]

Ask yourself if your daily choices demonstrate that you desire to go forward *together* as a couple, or if they indicate that you are following an independent course. When your husband is grumpy and cantankerous or depressed, following his lead can be a challenge. Rise to the occasion with all your creativity and intelligence. Be determined not to give up on winning his heart when your first attempts go awry. Successful people never give up. Successful marriages are built on commitment and perseverance.

If women will commit themselves to practicing biblical submission, they will strengthen generations to come. Consider the words of Richard Strauss:

> When Dad abdicates his position of authority in the home, Mom usually assumes the role she was never intended to have. The unhappy combination of a disinterested father and an overbearing mother can drive children to run away from home, enter early and unwise

marriages, or suffer emotional difficulties and personality deficiencies. Dad must take the lead. . . . A dominant wife and mother confuses the children. . . . If mothers and fathers have equal authority, the child does not know which one to obey. He will use the one against the other to get his own way, and will soon lose respect for one or both parents. Studies have shown that children with conduct problems often have domineering, high-strung mothers. But if a child knows beyond all doubt that Dad is the head of the house, that Mom speaks for Dad, and that Dad's authority backs up what she says, he will be more apt to obey and will have more love and respect for both his parents.[5]

In this age of domestic abuse, I must add a note of caution: Biblical support and submission does *not* mean accepting abuse. Any woman who is living in a physically abusive marriage must pursue help. Do not enable destructive behavior. Consider consulting James Dobson's book *Love Must Be Tough* for guidelines.[6]

## Create a Positive Feeling in His Heart

Physical expressions of affection, more than anything, can touch a man's heart. Those gentle touches, along with a smile and look of admiration, have an impact. So does the sight and smell of good food when he's tired and hungry.

Positively reinforce your husband regularly. When he's feeling good about himself, he will more likely feel good about you. Praise him in front of your children. Talk him up to the children. Tell others how you appreciate your husband.

Ask questions about how he's feeling and then listen to his answers. Share your own concerns so you develop intimacy. Passivity erects emotional walls in your relationship. No one can guess what's going on in another person's head. Be assertive about sharing feelings in a nonthreatening manner. Instead of pointing an accusing finger when he doesn't follow through on something he said he'd do, say, "I am feeling disappointed." This kind of honest statement is a lot more inviting than complaining, "You blew it! You never do what you say you'll do!"

Show your husband that he pleases you. No doubt you can think of his numerous shortcomings and how you'd like to see him change, but if you'll just accept him with a smile, you'll do both of you a favor. He can literally come alive from your praise and acceptance and renew all those positive feelings you once had.

# Actively Promote Communication

Promoting communication is part of relational maintenance. We cannot expect a relationship to stay strong if we deprive it of nourishment. In fact, we can cause it to suffocate if we don't keep the channels of communication open.

Knowing how to foster communication in marriage and families is critical, yet many people are ignorant of the necessary skills. Few of us take classes in high school or college on improving communication, yet we communicate every day. We would be wise to cultivate good communication skills before the misunderstandings in our relationships have destroyed us.

Our attitude and approach toward our husbands can either promote or discourage further interaction and communication. When I talk with Stu about concerns that are important to me, I try to remember that he'll hear me better if I speak in a safe and positive way. If I help him feel good about himself through my positive demeanor, we set a more friendly, compatible context in which to discuss the issue. Whether or not you believe you need help with communication, I recommend attending the FamilyLife marriage or parenting conference. For more information about these seminars, write for a free conference brochure: FamilyLife, 3900 North Rodney Parham, Little Rock, AR 72212. Or call 1-800-FL-TODAY (1-800-358-6329).

# Show Him Respect

Respect is a biblical mandate. Ephesians 5:33 says, "The wife must respect her husband" (NIV). The Amplified Bible translates this, "Let the wife see that she respects and reverences her husband—that she notices him, regards him, honors him, prefers him, venerates and esteems him; and that she defers to him, praises him, and loves and admires him exceedingly."

We honor God as we fulfill His command to respect our husband throughout all the seasons of our marriage, be they good, bad, or ugly. So build up your husband. Be the one who makes him feel like a million bucks. His ego needs it, and both of you will profit more than you can imagine. Try it.

If you feel resistant to this idea, you might consider why. Is it selfishness on your part? Maybe his choices in life don't seem to merit your respect. If so, remember that God doesn't hold you responsible for your husband's choices, but He does expect you to respect your husband as a person. I encourage you to step out in faith and tell your man how wonderful he is. Find the positive. Compliment him repeatedly. You may have to call a rescue squad to pick him up off the floor, but you'll certainly be a winner.

The Bible tells us that women can win their husbands without a word. First Peter 3:1–2 says, "Wives, in the same way be submissive to your husbands so that, if any of them do not believe the word, they may be won over without words by the behavior of their wives, when they see the purity and reverence of your lives" (NIV).

Wow! What an opportunity we have to influence our husbands for the Kingdom! We also have a responsibility to behave in ways that can win them. Stop and let this concept sink in so you can take concrete steps to activate it. Ask yourself, *Am I good at showing respect? How can I do this? What can I genuinely compliment him for?*

Your husband needs to feel that you respect his leadership. Be alert to ways you can influence him, but let him take the lead. Even if something was your idea, he'll feel good about being able to proceed as you enthusiastically follow and praise him for each step he takes. Let him feel good about being a leader. Don't give in to the temptation to take over, even if you are more capable in a certain area.

In our house, I keep the financial books. This was a decision we made together because I enjoy the job more than Stu does. But our marriage in general is under Stu's leadership. We both give input on decisions, but the final say—and responsibility—rests with him.

Part of respecting your husband's leadership is trying *not* to be his mother. You are not his conscience; you are the person who can point him to higher ground by demonstrating respect for his leadership, publicly and privately.

# Be Aware of the Unique Stresses in Your Lives

Keep your eyes open so you're always aware of ways to maintain and improve your marriage. Left unattended, what God has joined together may fall apart. You'll need to build fortresslike walls around weak areas so your relationship doesn't crumble.

First, be aware of the family of origin each of you came from and what frame of reference you each bring to life. Experts tell us that we live out as adults what we learned at home as children. For example, does either of you come from a strong conservative background? As a result of those years of restraint, could either of you be harboring unconscious desires for "freedom"?

Also be aware of the potential for relational chemistry, that is, to the dynamics that can develop between men and women, specifically your husband and other women, or you and other men. Lack of awareness causes many Christian marriages to be threatened.

Dennis Rainey discusses the dangers of emotional adultery:

> High school chemistry taught me a very valuable lesson. When certain substances come into close contact, they can form a chemical reaction. I proved that one day during my senior year of high school when I dropped a jar full

of pure sodium off a bridge into a river and nearly blew up the bridge. You'd think that I would have at least had enough sense to have stepped off the bridge! What I've learned since then is that many people don't respect the law of chemistry any more than I did back then. They mix volatile ingredients without giving much thought to the explosion which could occur. I've discovered that many married people don't understand that a chemical reaction can occur with someone other than their mates. Don't misunderstand me here—I'm not just talking about sexual attraction; I'm referring to a reaction of two hearts, the chemistry of two souls. This is emotional adultery—an intimacy with the opposite sex outside the marriage. Emotional adultery is unfaithfulness of the heart. When two people begin talking of intimate struggles, doubts or feelings, they may be sharing their souls in a way that God intended exclusively for the marriage relationship. Emotional adultery is friendship with the opposite sex that has progressed too far. Often it begins as a casual relationship at work, school, even church. A husband talks with a female co-worker over coffee and shares some struggles he's facing with his wife or kids. She tells of similar problems, and soon the emotions ricochet so rapidly that their hearts ignite and can ultimately become fused together as one. To those who've experienced it, this catalytic bonding seems too real to deny.[7]

As you work to guard your marriage, I recommend that you read *The Snare* by Lois Mowday Rabey.[8] She helps readers understand the emotional and sexual entanglements that are subtly but powerfully overtaking many good but inappropriately involved people.

Reading books like this will keep us educated about human tendencies during various seasons of life. Some behaviors are predictable, and being aware of them can help us prevent trouble. Recognize your personal responsibility and exercise it. We can't be responsible for our husband's choices, but our own actions can strongly encourage specific behavior in him, positively or negatively. When your husband is being swayed by a coworker's intellectual stimulation, flattery, generosity, or by coy nonverbal expressions, are you asking what you are doing to help counteract that by your own pursuit of his attention?

Be aware of your own vulnerable times as well, and take godly measures to safeguard your mind, body, and spirit. Perhaps you are newly married and wonder if you've made a big mistake. Every other man may look better than the one you have. When the last child leaves the nest all day for school or college, you may unconsciously seek affirmation from others. Or maybe a death, job loss, or move to another state has left you feeling lost and lonely. When working through some of these issues, professional counseling is often useful. Don't be afraid to seek help. In the process, remember that things usually have to get worse (or feel worse) before they get better, as the issues are laid bare. Do keep turning to God. Remember, you can make it!

# Make Sure He Has Reason to Admire You

Do you have qualities that naturally draw your husband to you? Which list below most accurately describes you? And how many negative traits are you willing to work at changing?

| Negative | Positive |
|---|---|
| Selfishly oriented | Unselfishly oriented |
| Distant/aloof | Able to be intimate |
| Demanding | Giving |
| Doubting | Trusting |
| Confused | Wise |
| Wavering | Loyal |
| Deceptive | Honest |
| Avoids responsibility | Takes responsibility |

| | |
|---|---|
| Complainer | Joyful |
| Exaggerating | Truthful |
| Impatient | Patient |
| Defensive | Teachable |
| Makes assumptions | Grateful |
| Explosive | Peaceful |
| Rigid | Flexible |
| Driven | Balanced |
| Destructive | Nurturing |

As you look at the positive list, which qualities first attracted him to you? Do those qualities still characterize you? It takes work to cultivate a positive outlook and behavior. Are you willing to invest the effort?

# The Legacy of a Strong Marriage

When we work hard to develop depth in our marriage, we are prepared to offer our children the gift they need most: a model for their future.

Confident children don't just materialize. That twenty-year window of nurturing and modeling lends a great opportunity to shape lives for generations to come. We are building a legacy. When we recognize the thousands of things we do at home as messages we're sending our children about their importance and value, we can feel honored. We're not wasting our time; we're helping the next generation become solid citizens in a society that lacks purpose and direction. What a role we have!

As you seek to warm the hearts in your home by encouraging your husband and helping to build a strong marriage, you will enjoy his pleasure and have assurance that you've provided your children with a rich heritage. God's character is reflected and His reputation can shine. Everybody wins.

# PART 3

# Facet #2

# Nurturer Meant to Develop

## CHAPTER 8

# *The Nurturing Process*

*I* remember a slogan that a company used years ago: "Progress is our most important product." Obviously, they valued their end product or they wouldn't be in business, but they weren't satisfied with just producing a product. They continually wanted to improve that product.

Is this how we look at the nurturing process? Or are we hoping for some great product and yet disregarding the incredible work that the process requires? In order to reflect any light through this feminine facet, we must learn to view nurturing as a process.

We live in an "instant" society. We expect results now. With the least effort possible, we want to get dinner ready in seconds, to get thin quickly, to get out of debt tomorrow, to be a skillful athlete or musician instantly, to have a great marriage immediately, and of course, to have well-behaved, confident children from their birth.

# Early Stages to More Advanced

A nurturing process takes place in any situation where the development of something or someone is fostered from an early stage to a later, more advanced level. A woman effectively nurtures in many realms. She may care for the elderly, do gardening, care for pets, visit a widow, rescue the neighbor's toddler from the street and then develop a friendship, or teach children's Sunday school for thirty years. Nurturing isn't limited to caring for our own children. Opportunity presents itself in every area God places us.

However, nurturing children is the complex process on which we will focus in this section. Just because a woman stays at home doesn't automatically indicate that she is nurturing her children.

Eve, as the mother of all living (Gen. 3:20), left her daughters a noble heritage. She and Adam were commanded in Genesis 1:28 to "be fruitful and multiply, and fill the earth, and subdue it." From the time they are born, children are like the black and white lines in a coloring book. They need filling in. On a basic level, it is relatively easy to ensure their physical development. But there are other spaces to fill. Because these spaces exist out of sight, they can be difficult to nurture. Yet it is those "interior" spaces that give a child's life dimension. As mothers we are artists, whether we realize it or not. We shape the future of our children and of our society by how we "color" those spaces. Being an effective "colorer" takes all the intelligence and understanding we can gather. It also demands a good attitude and a proper perspective as we remember "children are a gift of the LORD; / The fruit of the womb is a reward" (Ps. 127:3).

It would be helpful if the Bible included one lengthy book presenting easy step-by-step instructions in nurturing. However, it seems that God deemed it a fruitful experience for us to gather principles from throughout Scripture to acquire the understanding we need. Proverbs 28:5 says, "But those who seek the LORD understand all things."

When our children come with homework questions about geometry theorems and chemical equations, those subjects may be beyond our immediate grasp. We will have to dig through the textbook to refresh our memory before we can help with the problem.

Likewise, God will grant wisdom to those who dig in the Scriptures and pursue a relationship with Him. The understanding that God wants to give us is the ability to nurture, to discern the intents of our child's heart, to make fair parenting decisions, and to set firm boundaries. With the stakes so high, we must fill our mental reservoir with skillful tips and principles of wisdom from God. We can't know too much to nurture a child well.

# We Can't Know Too Much

When most of us face a medical procedure, we want to know everything we can about it. I also want the doctor with the most expertise in this field to help me. I want this individual to have seen and effectively treated this need before. My doctor can't know too much when he or she is dealing with my concern. The same is true with the molding of our children's lives. The more we know, the better.

When it comes to mothering, a great deal of skill and intelligence is required to succeed. Read books about mothering, listen to tapes, and watch other mothers nurture. Adopt the good and reject the bad. As we apply creativity, energy, and skill to our extensive undertakings, our family can't help but win.

We want to channel the talents we might possess and the learning we have acquired into enhancing our child's thinking, attitudes, and actions. No experience as a single woman is wasted. Each and every circumstance in our past fills a reservoir from which we can draw lessons for our children or for the children of others. May we all feel privileged to influence these precious lives as we muster all our qualifications toward their growth. Learning to nurture children is a lifelong process.

# The Need Is Great

From an unnamed parent whose teen took his life after a season of using drugs, we hear these words, "Please, do whatever it takes to get between your child and drugs."

A grandmother, whose five-year-old grandson was pushed out of a fourteenth-story window to his death by troubled boys, says this, "We hope that somebody—somewhere, somehow—will do something about the conditions which are causing our children to kill each other."[1]

From parents whose teens have either committed suicide or deliberately shot and killed people around them, we hear a similar anguished cry: "We don't understand why this happened. We did everything possible for that child." That phrase, "everything possible," points to just how great a child's needs are and why we must develop our opportunities to lead and encourage our children.

# Inadequate Attempts to Color the Spaces

Obviously we have some differences of opinion about what nurturing means in our society. Too many legislators believe that pumping money into more child-care facilities will provide for our children. Many parents believe that baby-sitters and material things are all that kids really need. One famous movie star made a statement that betrays her unperceptive heart. Rationalizing her ability to continue fulfilling her multimillion-dollar movie contract and caring for the child she was adopting, she announced that all she needed to raise a child was a room, a few toys, and a baby-sitter.

I simply cannot passively accept these views. The impact we have as moms upon society is far too great for silence to be mistaken for acquiescence. Discovering what it takes to positively nurture the next generation is a crucial step in helping children reach their potential. And when our products—these precious children—are at their best, we experience exhilaration. If only we would "buy" this answer, instead of spending billions of misplaced dollars on temporary and doomed "fixes." Imagine how many lives we could change.

What is the big secret that will unlock the doors to strengthening society and unleashing the feminine ability to nurture? The answer lies in the principle of Galatians 6:7: "For whatever a man sows, this he will also reap." Although there can be natural disasters along the way, the law of the harvest remains. What we put into our children affects how they grow and mature. We parents need to focus on the principle of personal responsibility of sowing and all that the nurturing process entails.

# The Tree Analogy

Because I grew up amidst orchards in Yakima, Washington, I watched year-round as farmers faithfully tended their trees. They never quit. They were always doing something to maintain their crops. The value of a healthy tree is far reaching; therefore the ongoing process remains important.

The promise of a healthy product and, thus, an income for the next year motivated their work. They didn't complain that it took too long or that each phase was unimportant. They didn't take long breaks or neglect any measures, no matter how small. Farmers remained acutely aware of the consequences they'd experience. Their drive and actions are a good model of the commitment of mothers. And the value of the farmers' healthy trees goes on for generations as well.

I pray that you will recognize the importance of nurturing and intensify your efforts. Obviously things don't just happen. Products don't just appear without very careful provision. *Provision* means to supply or furnish. Its etymological roots lie significantly in the Latin *pro-video* meaning to "look ahead." The farmer and the nurturing mom alike need to stay healthy if they are to look ahead for their products to come. By "provisioning," you can anticipate and fulfill your child's needs by understanding and administering your own sense of process.

I hope you will study the "Process Required for Product" chart on the next page. As you contemplate the immense work needed, I pray that your appreciation for details will be enhanced. And I also pray that you choose to be involved at the highest level.

As our farmer friend John says of his tree crop, "The value is in the roots. When the roots are healthy, the tree can fight off disease and be strong." The farmer must provide the right care, support, protection, and timing. (See the tree illustration.) In each area, the process requires attention to a myriad of details. If any link in the process is omitted, those

# Process Required for Product

## The Farmer
### must provide the RIGHT:

**Care** - *soil prep, planting, cultivating, watering*

**Support** - *staking, fertilizing, inspecting*

**Protection** - *weeding, pruning, spraying, smudging*

**Timing** - *thinning, propping, picking (not by the almanac)*

## To meet the crop's needs at just the RIPE moment

## The Nurturing Mom
### must provide the RIGHT:

**Care** - *dimensionally (physical, mental, emotional, and spiritual)*

**Support** - *solid foundation, a discerning parent, connection, a training plan*

**Protection** - *boundaries/hedges, supervision, advice, prevention procedures, discipline*

**Timing** - *"scheduled availability" during windows of opportunity*

## To meet the child's needs at just the RIPE moment

*If the farmer is not there ... there is not much hope for a great harvest*

*If mom is not there ... serious deficiencies affect the harvest of character and self-esteem*

## *What quality of product are we ensuring?*
### *(barring flood, freeze, or conditions beyond our control)*

© 1999 Linda Weber

foundational roots suffer devastating effects. The consequences then affect the farmer's product. Ignoring or improperly handling the process will cause painful loss.

The chart illustrates the nuances of meaning behind Proverbs 22:6: "Train up a child in the way he should go, / Even when he is old he will not depart from it." (The Hebrew meaning of *train* is, "the continual active initiation of life boundaries.") A great deal of effort lies behind the instruction of this verse. Nurturing is serious business that produces long-term effects for society.

# The Nurturing Mom Is Like the Farmer

Mom's nurturing process also requires just the right *care, support, protection*, and *timing*. When she develops this process, she can meet deep needs and enable proper character and self-esteem development. Without doubt, practicing the process affects the quality of the product.

When my boys were young, I worked at maintaining physical proximity with positive vibrations. I smiled at them, touched them, and gave them "high fives." I labored "to be around" so I could compliment them at every opportunity. As they got older, I simply demonstrated the same principles in a more sophisticated fashion. I wanted them to know in their minds and experience in their hearts that I really loved them.

## The Right Care

*The Physical Realm.* The nurturing mom makes sure she is caring for her children dimensionally. Operating in the physical realm is only the beginning. Before we continue, I want to mention a few specifics. A woman's touch in preparing food for her household is unfortunately becoming a lost art. Proverbs 31:14–15 speak about this fine woman bringing food from afar and rising while it is still night to get food for her household. Interestingly, the builder of our house recently noted that the trend regarding ovens in homes reflects an increase in microwaves and a decrease in conventional ovens. Why? Regular home-cooked meals are losing out to the individual frozen box meal. Nurturing through preparing family meals is being lost.

In Scripture so much of what is really important takes place around the table. Woe to us who underestimate the value that comes from preparing and sharing food together. It is another art for women to identify and develop. Most of all, we can follow the Lord's example: "And Thou dost give them their food in due time" (Ps. 145:15).

Caring for the physical realm (food, clothing, health, and safety), like any category of life, should be done in balance. Too little physical care reflects abuse or selfishness when we consistently ignore the needs of our family in favor of our own. Overindulgence, on the other hand, is just as destructive; we spoil our kids. Too many material provisions decrease children's appreciation for the benefits of work and lower their incentive to provide a few things for themselves. Pushing a child into physical perfection (demanding the best in looks, the top spot at beauty pageants, athletic or music competitions, etc.) no matter how well intentioned, counteracts all healthy nurturing. The right balance of physical care is needed. Yet there is so much more that affects the heart and spirit.

As I've had the opportunity to teach women the art of nurturing, I have developed the following diagram to help answer the question "Am I nurturing my child beyond the obvious physical realm?" (See chart on page 106.) In mothering circles, this question is far more important than what people are usually asking, "Are you a working mom?" Although it is a simple diagram, if the reality of it were caught and lived, it would provide a healthy society. "Says easy, but does hard," as the saying goes.

There are a lot of incredibly intelligent people who act on what they see with their eyes only. They make sure their children have the externals, but they overlook the underlying mental, emotional, and spiritual realms.

*The Mental Realm.* When we delve beneath the surface of our children's needs, we find the mental realm. Many theorize that I can affect my child's IQ, interests, and abilities by reading to him with specific kinds of input. My child's intelligence is developed in direct proportion to the amount of live language he receives. The year my husband was in Vietnam, I enjoyed practicing this concept with our eight-month-old son, Kent. With all that extra time, I worked to activate the principles I found in the book *Give Your Child a Superior Mind.* I'll never know what specific good

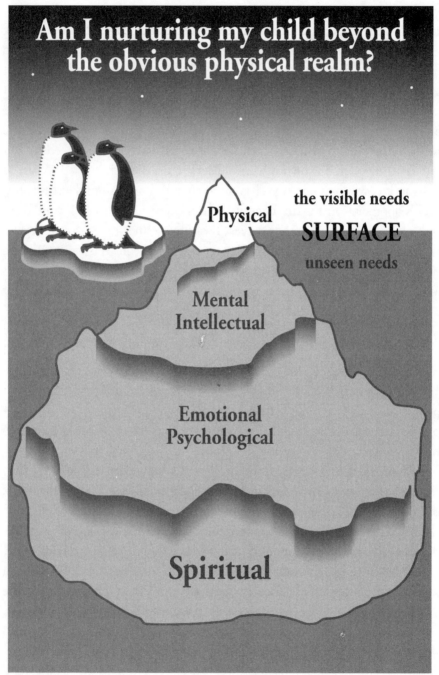

# Am I nurturing my child beyond the obvious physical realm?

Physical

the visible needs

**SURFACE**

unseen needs

Mental
Intellectual

Emotional
Psychological

Spiritual

© 1999 Linda Weber

my efforts did, but Kent now holds an undergraduate degree and graduate degrees from Durham and Oxford Universities in England.

*US News and World Report* notes the importance of nurturing the mental realm:

> According to recent findings, the neuron links that are the keys to creativity and intelligence in later life are mainly laid down by the age of three. Is inherited ability the main factor in establishing this connection? Apparently not. Interactions with an attentive adult—in most cases, a mother—matter most. In their book *Meaningful Differences in the Everyday Experience of Young American Children*, professors Todd Risley and Betty Hart say that the number of words an infant hears each day may be the single most important predictor of later intelligence and economic and social success.[2]

Many moms work to teach their children their ABCs early. It makes parents feel proud to see this happen before the neighbor's kids learn theirs—as if this matters. What really matters is the child's total development, and Mom actively plays an irreplaceable part in encouraging bright children.

*The Psychological/Emotional Realm.* While all kinds of provisions for superior educational opportunities are invaluable, an even deeper level of need may remain unnurtured. Because many aspects of a child's identity exist internally, we parents often possess a blind spot when it comes to these "unseen" dimensions. Yet the psychological/emotional level of need is where a significant opportunity lies.

We have the option of developing the hearts and spirits of our children by the words we say to them and the messages we send them through our body language and our tone of voice. We can prevent or patch up emotional holes in our children's hearts through developing the art of nurturing. It takes a lot of unselfish creative work to do it right. And our actions speak volumes.

Let's talk about the heart. Both the physical and the emotional heart are unseen. In both cases, the heart pumps lifeblood to all areas of the body and brings depleted cells to be reoxygenated. Each one needs to be fed, nurtured, and exercised to grow and pump efficiently. Keeping each one strong is essential to the essence of life.

When our awareness is heightened, we will find pleasure in doing those seemingly lesser things that, in fact, strengthen the child's inner being. Care of the emotional heart allows healthy fruit to be produced. What is flowing out of the heart at your house?

All my boys have blessed my heart with special expressions of how they've felt cared for beyond the physical realm. Kent surprised me with this note recently.

> Over so many opportunities, you "chose" to be my mom first. Bless you for this, Mom! Please believe me, it has made ALL THE DIFFERENCE. Mom, cheers to you for pouring yourself into me like you have. Thank you for loving me into the person I am and for a thousand special touches: for sending Dad my kiddy books in Vietnam so his taped voice could read to me, for French toast on game days, for being there EVERY game and EVERY time I came home, for morning glimpses of you in the Scriptures, and for your CONSTANT affirmations. Mom, I feel so lucky in everything I do, and I owe so much of this to you. Your love has endowed me with the confidence, the fearlessness, and the optimism that no kid should go without. You have certainly made some sacrifices to give me what I have, and I just want you to be reminded how much you are loved for all you do. Mom, I am so honored, humbled, and proud to be your son.

While on an airplane, I got into a conversation with the man next to me about nurturing. He noted how his neighbors have three children and yet they don't take time to raise them. "My wife and I have only two children," he said, "but we spend time with them, helping them feel loved and cared for." Good observation.

Raising children does take time and effort. After caring for our young children during a long trip we made to Israel years ago, my mother-in-law said, "The true miracle in the biblical Sarah's life was not her conception during old age, but rather her ability to raise the children as an older woman." Caring for each realm simultaneously requires much.

Making strong connections emotionally prevents possible power outages later. A kid can totally fall apart if we fail to fortify the fuse box and wiring system.

*The Spiritual Realm.* Delving further, we reach the most important aspect of a child's development—a spiritual foundation. Without a relationship with Jesus Christ and following the design of the Creator who knows best, we live a self-oriented life without true wisdom or direction. Nurturing the spiritual dimension in our children is the most important job we could ever have.

Without a foundation, any house crumbles. Without spiritual development, our lives are not only incomplete but also destined for trouble, to put it mildly. When you follow the nurturing opportunities described in Deuteronomy 6:4–9 (when you walk by the way, when you sit down, and when you rise up), you can help your children learn to know and live out the principles of God. Reading bedtime stories and saying prayers together are two natural times to share spiritual tidbits. Driving your kids to the orthodontist, ball practices, or music lessons is a great time for conversation. Maybe your nurturing input will come while putting a puzzle together or helping on school projects.

Whenever our children mention fears or worries, we can point them to the ultimate comfort of Christ. One mother whose child had frequent bad dreams used the opportunity to pray with her child, asking God's comfort and help in replacing the bad thoughts with good ones. Confidently and continually the mother helped the child to stay in her own bed, teaching the child to trust and believe in God's watchful care. What an incredible opportunity we have when we are side-by-side with these wonderful children during this twenty-year window of time.

We will affect our children's physical, emotional, and spiritual realms either positively through our conscious development or negatively through neglect. God made woman with a desire to nurture. Embrace your opportunities to pour your life into nurturing the children of the next generation, whether they are your own or someone else's children.

When it comes time for our life on this earth to be complete, we will die. What legacy will we leave? We can't take possessions or titles or the like with us. By nurturing the next generation, we send secure lives—whose hearts reflect the love they've been given—out to impact their world. Through their lives our influence affects generations. Thank you, Lord, for such a privilege of influence that will make a difference to a world I'll never know personally.

## The Right Support

*A Solid Foundation.* A support system begins with a solid foundation. Recently I was having lunch with my son Ryan, who works in the commercial construction world. We discovered concepts in building foundations which are easily transferred to the work of a nurturing mom. Ryan told me how you could pour cement all day long, yet if adequate steel reinforcements were not stabilizing that cement, the least rumble or disturbance would cause destruction.

So much more critical in life is assuring our children's internal foundational development—emotionally and spiritually. We can "pour cement all day" by telling them to pick up their toys, clean their rooms, stop fighting with their sister, and eat more vegetables. But if the "steel reinforcements" of the knowledge of God's love and care and our love and care are not there when they encounter a disturbing circumstance, their façade will crumble.

*A Discerning Parent.* Providing support emotionally requires you to be a discerning mom. Hebrews 5:13–14 helps us see that maturity is developed for those "who because of practice have their senses trained to discern good and evil." Like working out in a gym, we can "work out our mind" in the Word of righteousness to be a discerning nurturer. Proverbs 31:26 describes this type of nurturer: "She opens her mouth in wisdom, / And the teaching of kindness is on her tongue." In a very broad description, that same Proverbs passage (v. 27) goes on to refer to this nurturer's support work: "She looks well to the ways of her household, / And does not eat the bread of idleness." Thousands of actions translate into messages of emotional support.

Part of a woman's discernment is to distinguish how each child is gifted and how she might best channel these gifts. Writing about the influence of her mother, Ingrid Trobisch quotes her mother, Mutti, as saying, "'Look! That child is like a budding flower; every day a new petal unfolds.' From her sensitivity I learned to recognize one child's artistic nature, another's love for music, another's gift for hospitality. She helped me ask the right questions to bring out their different personalities."[3]

The discerning mom can further her abilities to nurture her child emotionally by taking advantage of support groups. I've been the advisor to a mom-to-mom group at our church for nine years. Watching these women gain understanding and encourage each other's perseverance with their children gives pleasure to my soul. I recommend that you find a group, read books on personality traits and talents, and maybe take a class to maximize your efforts. Everybody will win.

A *Training Program*. To give birth to a child and then simply hope he makes it in life is preposterous. To ensure the quality formation of good attitudes, responses, and patterns for living, mom faces the greatest challenge ever. When dad comes home and wonders what she has been doing all day, she can simply respond, "I've been building the next society."

Part of producing a good product requires *ensuring* a training program. In keeping with the spirit of Romans 10:14, how can one learn except he be taught? That's what process is all about—we have to teach children what they need to know.

Gary Bauer says, "Children must be taught reliable standards of right and wrong. After all, they only know what you teach 'em."[4] This is where mentoring comes in. Those kids are watching every move we make. Children are little tape recorders playing back all kinds of things they hear from us. They are also ongoing copy machines, which are producing duplicate copies of everything they observe in us. Scary, wouldn't you say? Little eyes and ears are always learning how to live life.

Besides modeling good behavior, we may also ask the Lord to show us the particular character traits or virtues He wants us to work at instilling in that child during a particular year. If we have a goal, a character quality of the year, we will be more likely to make progress than if we try to instill all qualities at once in a hit-or-miss style. We don't want to overwhelm our children with an intensive crash course. On the other hand, if we have no plan, our children use the default method of learning—they catch whatever is around them. When we allow someone else to do the modeling, we can lose control of the end result.

Our attitudes, responses, and patterns are being observed. Our words and our tone of voice, facial expressions, and other body language are being practiced. Unfortunately, our bad habits as well as our good ones are picked up. How we get along with others is usually prophetic of how our children will get along in life. We should make a conscientious effort not to pass on manipulative controlling tendencies, a victim orientation, or a negative or dishonest spirit.

Besides reliable standards of right and wrong, our children need to understand that excellence requires effort on their part. Great results don't just happen for us or for them. We need to praise their beginning attempts, regardless of the final outcome. As we provide a myriad of materials and opportunities, our child is free to try a project and develop a sense of accomplishment.

One of my favorite pictures of the kids is of Kent and Blake when they were six and four years old, making an airplane out of scrap lumber. I was probably stretching the safety factor by allowing boys that age to use a hammer and nails, but the product they came up with was amazing. I never would have dreamed they could do so well. The project ended up being prophetic for Blake, as he is now flying his own plane.

Somewhere in a child's nurturing process he or she needs to be encouraged to venture out and explore by learning and doing. Sandy Lynam Clough says this:

> A hobby can help children explore their personal interests and develop their unique talents and abilities. Children who do not know how to do anything may depend too much on the media for entertainment, but children who

have learned to be creative and how to work with their hands are never bored. A hobby can be an adventure in learning traditional skills, discovering the joy of creating, and experiencing the deep satisfaction that comes with finishing a job. A hobby is a gift we give to our children, a gift that keeps on giving pleasure.[5]

The extensiveness and kinds of training available are limitless, proving the old maxim that the more you put into something, the more you get out of it.

*Connection Is Key.* As with electricity, when there is connection there is power. This principle of connection is essential to the support a nurturing mom will give. Susan, who was a mother to seven- and nine-year-old girls and a vice president of a prominent bank in Atlanta, possessed "a growing desire to be more involved" with her children at this stage of their lives. She explained, "My first priority is to strengthen a bridge of communication before my girls enter the teen years. I want time to know them better, to be aware of their gifts so I can reinforce and guide them."[6]

I encourage you to realize the need for connection with your children from the very beginning. Your dedication to providing a lifeline of connection will affect all your child's future relationships. Consider this:

If the first relationship a baby has does not set the stage for trust, then later relationships cannot be based on trust. The baby learns from the first relationship what he can and cannot expect from others. If there is no healthy give and take, the baby will not know how to give and take with others. Unattached children do not grow socially. They have great difficulty learning to build any kind of relationship.[7]

My boy, Blake, a man now, wrote to me with these words of connection. In Blake's words, you can sense the value in what you, a mom, can do to support your children:

*My dear Mother,*

*I just wanted to thank you for so many things that you have done for me. Mom, you are truly the ultimate definition of mother. You mothered me day in and day out. I love you for caring, Mom! You shall never be forgotten or taken for granted in this heart. You taught me the basics that are musts to be a successful adult who has it all together. You always created that warm environment. You've done your work and completed your investment of time. I know your love will never lessen.*

*I'm grateful for your desire to stick with it, your desire to take criticism. You are a positive pumping factory! And I am so glad that I am one too. I just want to tell you, Mom, I am what I am because you never quit. To think of the commitment you put in is unbelievable, Mom. I love you and if no one else ever recognizes you for your work, I do. I thank you for the lifelong investment you made by training and shaping me. The love of my mother has made Blake be Blake. I love you—Mom, You're Awesome.*

Moms, your ultimate example of connection is the Lord God. Isaiah 66:13 says, "'As one whom his mother comforts, so I will comfort you.'" The Holy Spirit is to us what we are to our children. John 14:16–18, 26, and 27 tells us, He will be with us, will not leave us as orphans, will come to us will teach us all things, will bring to our remembrance all He said, and will leave peace with us. What an opportunity we have to connect to the strong support levels God has for us.

## The Right Protection

Do you remember the three little pigs? Each chose a different level of protection in the process of building his house—straw, sticks, and bricks. Scripture describes two kinds of people: ones who build their houses on the rock and ones who build on sand.

*Boundaries and Hedges.* Life is filled with choices. What level of protection are you choosing as a nurturing mom? Will you build a fortified fence at the top of a cliff? Or do you prefer running an ambulance service at the bottom of that cliff?

It is so much easier on everybody when a prevention plan securely protects the participants. Why pick up all the broken pieces in the aftermath when we could prevent the trouble by supplying adequate boundaries in advance?

When the children are young, it is obvious we should not to let them wander into a busy street, touch a hot stove, or get too close to the unprotected stairs. But the ability to instill boundaries becomes more difficult when it comes to what TV or movies they may watch, who their friends should be, or what balance of freedom they should enjoy.

*Supervision and Advice.* The extent you give yourself to this aspect of nurturing affects the product you are producing. What quality of supervision do you provide? Are you monitoring the hard choices they are facing and giving adequate advice?

I told my children frequently that God gave me to them as a parent to help them make some hard choices. For example, though my decision to break some of their friendships apart was not a popular one then, years later, the critics thanked me. Providing quality protection with careful boundaries enables you to reflect bright light through the facet of nurturing.

*Prevention.* Developing a philosophy of friendship and dating now, where you determine ahead of time exactly what is desired, will diminish your frustrations later. As the need arises then, rules and expectations won't appear arbitrary or unfair. The same principle can be applied to other milestones, such as driving or learning to spend money.

Teaching life skills (be responsible, be courteous, help your neighbor, and use time wisely, etc.) is like planting good seeds with a good fertilizer. Without this beginning effort, we must later spend time weeding instead of sowing or harvesting. We're making way for the positive so the negative doesn't take over. And don't forget the weed killer. If discipline doesn't take place, we've got an unruly product. Proverbs 29:15–16 says, "The rod and reproof give wisdom, / But a child who gets his own way / brings shame to his mother. / When the wicked increase, transgression increases." This involved process requires quality nurturing.

*Admonishing and Blessing.* Being overprotective or too permissive are both violations of a balanced child developer. Waiting on God and His wisdom again can cause our homes to be the wombs of protection that children deserve and are longing for.

This Mother's Day greeting from my twenty-three-year-old, Ryan, encourages all of us to know that our protective support matters to the future of each of our children.

*Dear Mom,*

*I just wanted to take a little time today and type out a little bit of how appreciative I am for you. It is great to be your son. Not a day goes by that I am not thankful for you. Indeed I'm a blessed individual.*

*I cannot remember a day growing up when you were not there to tell me I was doing a good job and to protect from dangers that were unknown to my feeble little growing mind. What a blessing it is to have been protected from so much as a little child. Thank you very much, Mom.*

*Your determination to see that we grew up safe and healthy is very much appreciated. I cannot say enough, Mom. I love you so much, and I am so thankful for you. I hope you know and feel it.*

## The Right Timing

Have you noticed how we sometimes wait until something gets bad before we finally attend to it? Maybe a tooth that was sensitive starts killing you, the dryer that made strange noises quits totally, or the drippy faucet becomes a running stream?

With the nurturing process, we never know when a key moment will happen. "The big question" or a desperate need for help can't be predicted. Unfortunately, big moments come and go so quickly that we need to be mentally prepared with "scheduled availability" to be able to meet those deep needs at the right moment. By being available, we can make a big difference. Sometimes we can change a situation completely.

My children are helping to write this chapter on nurturing. Their insights into the expressions of nurturing may encourage you in making time to be available.

Mom,

*What a blessing to be your son. Every aspect of my life has been shaped by your devotion. You have taught me that complaining is not justified no matter how bad the circumstances; you have taught me that life isn't lived best with the abundance of possessions. You have demonstrated perseverance and even long suffering with a smile on your face. Mother, your sacrifice is evident to me in so many areas and will manifest itself as blessings in generations to come. The times growing up when you were ALWAYS there to help me make the little decisions in life are not forgotten. For I have found that I now make the big decisions in my life through the template you established early on. Mother, I thank you for tireless devotion and endless sacrifice. I thank you for taking the struggles of life head on for us so that we might not be led astray.*

*I thank you very much for giving of yourself for us. You have done a wonderful job. I couldn't have wished for a better mother. I love you.*

*Mama's little helper, Ry*

# Conclusion

Is this complex process worth what it requires of us? We each must decide. Are you willing to pay the price for omissions in any category? Eventually, it boils down to what we are willing to do without.

The more we attend to the details of this process, the more opportunities we will discover. It's like the picture my dentist places on the ceiling above his chairs. No matter how many times I've observed that picture, I continue to see new details.

With your inborn nature to nurture, you can take your skills and develop a combination that achieves more than a good grade in life. My prayer is that I've given you tracks to run on that will enrich the quality of life of each of your nurtured ones.

You can use your gifts to influence our world. The power of nurturing gives wings to every flight. You've heard it said, "She who rocks the cradle rules the world." Proverbs 31:28 says, "Her children rise up and bless her."

Michelle Beaulaurier of Burlingame, California, one of nine children, wrote the following to her mother, who was questioning her own at-home value: "I would not be where I am today had you not been where you were! You were my support system, my encourager, my peace, and my challenger to go for it and to use my talents. You were always there to point out my special, God-given talents so that I could reflect upon them and put them into use!"[8]

Your ability to nurture makes good things happen. The impact of the nurturing mom's process creates an environment for good products in life (see the chart below.) Smile!

❧

# The Impact of a Nurturing Mom's Process

| | **Lead To** | **Which Result In** | **Which Promotes** |
|---|---|---|---|
| **Mom's 1000 Points of Action** (Continual active initiation of life boundaries*) **Demanding Time Talent & Energy** | Children Feeling: <br> • Important <br> • Accepted <br> • Cared for <br><br> The Formation of: <br> (good) <br> • Attitudes <br> • Responses <br> • Patterns | • Emotional security <br> • Positive self-esteem <br> • The enhancing of God's reputation <br> • The prevention of behavioral problems <br> • A healthy heritage | • A happy family <br> • Mom experiencing: pleasure hugs kisses smiles self-respect |

**(and exhaustion)**

*Hebrew meaning of *train* in "train up a child" in Proverbs 22:6               © *Linda Weber, 1999*

CHAPTER 9

# Feeling Nurtured
# or Not

$\mathcal{A}$s a beautiful feminine creature, you possess unique gifts to nurture, to reflect light in a dark world, and the ability to steer others from a negative existence to a positive experience. Helping others feel nurtured shows who you are as a woman, what you do well, and why it is so important.

When we understand that God created us to nurture, we can get rid of passive nurturing trends and, instead, actively mold a future society that gains strength from the touch we provide. Cultivating the awareness of our God-given ability can change our lives and all those around us.

I realize that, for many reasons, all women are not mothers. But all women are born to nurture—it's who we are. In God's economy, the general plan is that women give birth to the babies. Because birth is only the beginning, we proceed further to enhance our abilities to cause these little

119

ones to *feel* nurtured. A woman's fundamental nurturing opportunity is to take that life which God has given and nourish it to maturity and strength. The thrust of this chapter is dedicated to this cause.

The principle of maintenance means that after we give birth we take care of that little life in the best way possible. We begin with the assets we own and maximize their strengths. We learn what it means to truly love our children (see Titus 2:4). "And whatever you do in word or deed, do all in the name of the Lord Jesus, giving thanks through Him to God the Father" (Col. 3:17).

# What Can We Do?

My three sons are very different from each other. They each have wonderful qualities and special gifts that stand out. Had I pushed them toward getting the same awards, earning the same grades, and pursuing the same interests I would have done them a grave injustice. Each needed the freedom to be his own person. Sometimes moms only feel secure when they have forced their desires onto their children.

Before you become a mother, one of the best things you can do is to develop your own healthy self-esteem. After we become mothers, we need to be sure that the source of our self-esteem doesn't depend on our children. When we know who we are and seek guidance and reinforcement from the right places, we won't force our children into molds they were never designed to fill. Stop often and ask yourself, *Why is _____ so important? Am I forcing this child to do something so I look good?* Children gain power to be their best because we were free to give sacrificially of ourselves without stipulations. Sensing our fulfillment, they will model their own healthy self-esteem on ours.

Just as the flight attendant tells passengers to care for their own oxygen mask first, so too, we will be better capable of helping those around us as we first prepare ourselves. By focusing on our character and our spiritual and physical health, we will energize and replenish our ability to nurture. Our resulting sense of security becomes essential to our freedom and skill in developing our children well.

Our security empowers the child's heart to feel nurtured. This security deepens as we feel important, irreplaceable, and influential.

# Recognizing Our Importance Stimulates Good Nurturing

You are important because you ensure the nurturing process. Your giving has purpose. Anne Morrow Lindbergh lends insight into purposeful giving and thereby encourages us to create or stimulate feelings of a nurtured heart.

> Woman instinctively wants to give, yet resents giving herself in small pieces. . . . I believe that what woman resents is not so much giving herself in pieces as giving herself purposelessly. What we fear is not so much that our energy may be leaking away through small outlets as that it may be going "down the drain." *Purposeful* giving is not as apt to deplete one's resources; it belongs to that natural order of giving that seems to renew itself even in the act of depletion. The more one gives, the more one has to give— like milk in the breast.[1]

# Mom Is Irreplaceable

Moms are irreplaceable. Much research is available about "early attachment." For motivated learners, appendix A lists resources offering several quotes to begin your quest of understanding this subject better.

If this discussion helps a few families prevent some serious behavioral problems, I would be grateful. I do not wish to make a career woman feel badly. Yet it is imperative we have our eyes wide open to the consequences of the lack of nurturing. Research can help us understand how our children can be protected from disaster.

Behavior and attitude problems that surface are often linked with choices of leaving our children with some inadequate caregiver or a substandard facility. On the surface, day-care options look good. Susie and Johnny are becoming socially skillful. They get to interact with many children and are exposed to opportunities they could never have at home. But the results of parental rejection and abandonment color their behavior and all of their relationships to come, particularly close ones.

My mission is not to make women feel guilty for using child-care. My mother had to leave my little brother in someone's care while she worked. Bruce needed a place to go from the time he was born in order for Mom to cover our twenty-five-dollar-a-month rent (obviously very meager), plus what other basics she could provide.

Regardless or whether you work away from home, awareness of being ultimately irreplaceable provides motivation to be active in meeting your child's need to feel nurtured.

# Providing a Secure Base

When my own children were growing up, I wanted (based on their needs) to be home and to provide a secure base for them. Whenever I considered working more hours or got too involved in my own projects too often, I gained a glimpse of the kind of insecurity I knew I did not want them to feel permanently. I just did not feel good watching them cry or react in another way because of my choice to leave them for other projects.

I did not have all the research at my fingertips, but my maternal promptings convinced me to keep the continuity of security building in their hearts. And as I observe what difference it has made in their lives now as adults, I am so thankful I followed my heart.

Oh, we desperately needed the money I could have contributed. My husband was in graduate school, and we had a meager income. It is hard to believe we lived on $450 a month with two children, even in the early '70s. I knew what financial limitation meant. After four years of that, we jumped to the $8,000-a-year level (including benefits) with three children to support. And after that three-year experience, we started a church at the same $8,000-a-year income, but had $4,000 of benefits. This bleak financial picture went on for years, until our oldest son was graduating from high school.

While my kids were preschoolers, I wanted to make them feel secure by being around full-time. Then when they were in school, I took flexible jobs, enjoying full advantage of working and being available. When they arrived home, I was there too. I could feel then what a difference it made, and many years later they have reinforced that by their verbal responses and confident lives. Although it was difficult financially, I'm glad I chose what I did. Now the boys say they had everything they really needed.

# Mom Has Influence

Isn't the correlation interesting between how Mom feels about things and how the children end up feeling? Is our influence positive or negative? We choose our attitude. (And, of course, the children choose their responses in life as well.) Many moms have good intentions and yet are simply unaware of the nuances of nurturing that take place in the emotional, psychological, and spiritual realms. What specifically can we do to steer our influence into a positive direction? What will promote warm fuzzy feelings in our children? How can we extend ourselves and send messages of importance, acceptance, and care so that our children feel our love? And what might we be doing or not doing to give children negative feelings and negative behavior as well?

# The Results of Nurturing

The chart on page 124 will help us see at a glance our actions and the feelings they invoke. The left side deals with our positive development, leading children to feel nurtured. And the right side explains our passive choices, leading children to have negative feelings. Keen awareness can enhance our family's future.

As you look at the chart, identify your own profile. Let's start with the positive results you are pursuing when you nurture.

# NURTURED OR NOT?

## *What Do the Children FEEL?*

### *Which is your profile?*

**P O S I T I V E**

1. Nourishing, ensuring enrichment and closeness, adding building blocks, equipping, giving creatively

The child FEELS: worthwhile, valued, loved, cared for

2. Promoting development of family root systems, a child's trust, boundaries, letting go

The child FEELS: secure, guided, confident

3. Tuning in to heart needs, honoring individuality, getting real, having a "yes" face

The child FEELS: cared for, secure, wanted

4. Fostering, molding, training, rearing, giving what it takes, complimenting

The child FEELS: important, prepared, grateful, respected

5. Supporting by being available, listening, watching, feeling, sharing experiences, reaffirming, meeting unscheduled needs when load gets heavy and things are hard

The child FEELS: secure, important, accepted

6. Hovering over a completed process, honoring, participating with enthusiasm

The child FEELS: loved, valued, emotionally prepared, safe

**N E G A T I V E**

1. Hoping for the best, being distant, assuming all is well, actual abuse

The child FEELS: trampled, overshadowed, overlooked, abandoned, uncared for, afraid, desperate, powerless, shamed

2. Discouraging children, offering no responsibilities/consequences, being too permissive or too domineering/controlling, abusing child's right to be nurtured

The child FEELS: confused, wounded, insecure, emotionally scarred, betrayed, unstable

3. Too busy, tired, stressed, divided, selfish to attend to heart needs, downing everything

The child FEELS: angry, rejected, resentful, indifferent

4. Ignoring clues of deviance and pain, avoiding provision of wise counsel, neglecting emotional needs of the heart, allowing a silent destruction (like the frog boiling to death, one degree at a time)

The child FEELS: unimportant, depressed, poorly about self, apathetic, destructive

5. Needing to be elsewhere, distant, demonstrating disapproval, unaware, sharing only the residence, children left with adult responsibilities, giving kids substitute love (things), alienating them

The child FEELS: abandoned/haunted by emptiness, disapproved of, rejected

6. Absentee parent can't see a child's dying heart (the child even needs to make an appointment with the parent simply to ask a question)

The child FEELS: empty, sad, lonely, hopeless, isolated, explosive

# 1. Nourishing, ensuring enrichment and closeness, adding building blocks, equipping, giving creatively

### Nurturing Result –
### The child FEELS: *worthwhile, valued, loved, cared for*

We speak the language of love through the thousands of acts we perform. The things we do that expend our time, talent, and energy send messages to our children that they are important, accepted, and cared for. The acts themselves seem insignificant—a dry diaper applied; food prepared; a lap provided while reading a story; help for a sick child all night long; head lice exterminated; a wise response when they get a bad grade, don't make the team, wreck the car, lose your jewelry, or cause a large doctor bill. But these acts send messages the children receive. Such actions and the environment we've created are important to assure they feel loved. The positive messages we want to send are as follows: You are valuable, I care, you are special, and I really love you. This is the prize-winning recipe we must use regularly. Are you up for all this? The rewards are far-reaching.

I remember so many times when my boys had high fevers from ear infections or some virus. I'd hold them close and try to help them feel loved. Edith Schaeffer refers to the same kind of actions that generate good feelings in her book *What Is a Family?*

> For some people the memory of illness carries with it the memory of loving care, cool hands stroking the forehead, sponge baths in bed, clean sheets under a hot chin, lovely-flavored drinks, alcohol back rubs, medicine given methodically by the clock, flowers near the bed, curtains drawn when fever is hurting the eyes, soft singing of a mother's or father's voice during a sleepless night.[2]

This nurturing touch is like a ritual that adds stability to life. Ingrid Trobisch, in *Keeper of the Springs*, says, "Emotional comforts consist of familiar sounds and tactile experiences like the softness of Mother's breast, as well as predictable experiences like the dawn after every dark night. Ritual is an ancient tool to honor patterns in God's creation. It is a way to celebrate our lives, to create and to keep family feeling."[3]

My friend Linda Campbell taught school for years. She observed that the children who demonstrated good self-esteem and a lack of problems were those who had been taught life messages at home—wait your turn, listen carefully, follow instructions, be courteous, respect authority, and so forth. These are basic building blocks we must not assume are in place. They must be instilled for a productive life.

I have sixty-two photo albums covering our thirty-three years of marriage (and I'm six years behind in placing photos). I love pictures and consider them a valuable tool in remembering good experiences. Pictures can be used to help a child remember the good times, to reinforce something good that he did. What a fun way to double our efforts to instill good feelings—a self-esteem booster.

## 2. Promoting development of family root systems, a child's trust, boundaries, letting go

### Nurturing Result –
### The child FEELS: secure, guided, confident

Your children may take a family systems course in college someday, but where they really learn to parent is from you at home. The real teaching happens as described in Deuteronomy 6, the passage I always use when autographing *Mom, You're Incredible*. The principles of God are to be on our hearts, and we're to be teaching them to our families when we sit, walk, lie down, and rise up. Stephen R. Covey says, "Quite simply, parents today must raise their children 'inside-out' rather than 'outside-in.'"[4] There is a lot to teach, and there is a lot to learn from inside-out.

In the process of taking a family systems course in college, my son Kent was moved to write the following letter after evaluating his root system.

*I'm so thankful for you, Mom, and I deeply appreciate every minute you ever spent with me, every activity you gave up,*

*every concern, every provision, every sacrifice that you always*
*gave. I'm convinced that the dominant reason that I've grown*
*up, developed, and matured with so few problems and so many*
*advantages is because you always loved me and looked out for*
*me like you did.*

Regarding family root systems, the way you relate to your children is going to heavily color how they relate to others later. Consider this tip in regard to sons. "Raising a sexually secure boy requires care and attention from Mom. When a home has a warm and loving atmosphere, sexual hang-ups are less likely to develop. Parents do their children a favor by expressing affection to them and to each other in appropriate ways."[5] Mom's strong appreciation for men in general is a healthy part of a child's learning to appreciate family root systems.

Joan Shapiro helps us understand our influence with our sons. "For a man, his relationship with his actual mother, with all her personality characteristics, and all the circumstances of their life together will mold how he sees, feels, experiences, and reacts to women. This will influence his relationships with the other important women in his life."[6]

Dr. Shapiro also says this about a woman's nurturing opportunity: "She can make the world a sunny place or a dungeon. [A boy] will transfer this feeling onto other women. He will tend to experience them as the ones who can free or chain him."[7]

### 3. Tuning in to heart needs, honoring individuality, getting real, having a "yes" face

*Nurturing Result –*
**The child FEELS: cared for, secure, wanted**

In order to begin meeting needs of the heart, we have to study each of our children to discover just what each one might need. The pulse will be different from child to child. Our feminine antennas need to be sensitive to the hurts, disappointments, and injustices affecting our sweet ones. We'll need to tune into the rejection they're facing or the exhilaration they are experiencing so we can relate. Find out what the voids are and feel it with them. Then you can seize the moment and minister to them. Discover their interests and participate. Memories of your tuning in to their concerns will be vivid.

Ryan once shot a duck, which was being safely kept in our freezer. Even though he was back at college, outside Chicago, two thousand miles away, Ryan really wanted his duck so his friend J. R. could help him learn the art of taxidermy. Well, that thing would unthaw and become a royal mess if I had mailed it. So to bring elation to my boy's heart, I decided to hand carry this "treasure" when we flew from Oregon to the East Coast for a speaking engagement. Would you believe when we got to the airport, our plane through Chicago got cancelled and they rerouted us through Denver? "I'm sorry, but I have a special need to go through Chicago today," I told the ticket counter personnel. As I was thinking how I could preserve this pride and joy of a package, I caught sight of Nathan, a good family friend, who was in line behind us. I learned that he was going to Chicago. He happens to love Ryan too, and so Nathan was gracious enough to complete the job this mom began.

There are many things we can creatively come up with to enhance our children's lives with encouragement—special foods fixed to please, beds turned down, notes left on their pillows, and winks at them.

One of our sons liked to display his hat collection around his room. My son spaced all those hats at different intervals. Now I prefer symmetry, so his arrangement did not look good to me. Fortunately, I never made a big deal about his workmanship and about how he wanted them displayed. It was a "feel good" experience to let them stay that way.

## 4. Fostering, molding, training, rearing, giving what it takes, complimenting

### Nurturing Result –
### The child FEELS: important, prepared, grateful, respected

Our faithfulness to God's calling is a foundation we are laying for the generations to come. Our precious children's children will be playing the music you are now writing. Our work is to fill the treasure chest of our family's future. The nurturing we do now will pay out later.

I hesitated to share this unsolicited letter my son Ryan wrote during his sophomore year in college. It is so personal, but the power of its content reflects this message—a strong nurturing process does invoke strong feelings that affect generations. Maybe God can use this to fulfill Hebrews 10:24: "Let us consider how to stimulate one another to love and good deeds." May this possibly help you feel moved to pursue your nurturing process in an even greater way.

> *January 17, '95*
> *Mom,*
>
> *I was just sitting here today taking a break from studying and you came to mind. In fact so much came to mind that I thought I would be robbing both of us if I didn't let you know. I heard the other day that an infant learns its ability to trust between the ages of 0–18 months. I was thinking of my first 18 months and obviously I can't remember them. But the only possible picture that comes to mind is of you holding me. It seems that you probably didn't even set me down in that 18 months. It was a picture of love I can't even describe.*
>
> *Though I grew up without being betrayed by anyone and with no reasons to doubt or not to trust someone, I am convinced you are the one who taught me to trust. Your love for me has never been doubted. I thank you for loving me. Mom, I don't know how you could love so much. When I was a baby all I did was crap and cry, but you loved me with everything you had. It is a picture to me of our Savior's love. All I ever do is whine and cry. I give nothing to Him yet He loves me with absolutely everything He's got. Mom, your love for me is Christlike. Your love has been given nonstop without always receiving anything back.*
>
> *Your love for me teaches me about Christ's love. I can think of no better illustration of His love than yours. I thank*

*you for always expressing your love to me when I didn't always express mine for you. I don't know how I'm communicating, but I hope you understand what I'm saying. I love you so much. I wish I could tell ya but you are not home. I so badly hope you understand how much I love you.*

*It's kind of funny the one time I want to do something for you, you're not home. That's definitely not the scenario we're used to. I thank you for every sacrifice you've made for me in the past. Sometimes you may have thought we were taking them for granted and I know we did sometimes, but I want to thank you a million times over right now for all the times I did take you for granted. I'm convinced there isn't a mom anywhere like you. What you have done is so amazing. It goes completely against all natural desires of the self and serves others. There just aren't moms around like you. You are so incredibly unique and obviously a gift from God. Mom, a wife like you is a rare find. I hope I am as lucky as Dad.*

*I've got lots of work and I'd better get back to it. But I wanted to let you hear my heart. I'm sorry I haven't been the perfect son and I wish I could have been for your sake, but I guess that is just a bigger testimony about your love. There is no explanation for your love. It defies all human reason and all selfish desires. A love like yours is no doubt from the Lord.*

*Your Baby, Ryan*

# 5. Supporting by being available, listening, watching, feeling, sharing experiences, reaffirming, meeting unscheduled needs when load gets heavy/when things are hard

### Nurturing Result –
### The child FEELS: secure, important, accepted

Being available to your children may mean giving up your wishes and dreams for twenty years while you focus on their needs. If our children do not have easy access to our time and energy, the cost of trouble down the line can cause more than twenty years of heartache and negatively affect our descendants. Why? Availability breeds attention, which breeds affirmation, which breeds acceptance. This is the gift we give our child so he or she may become a solid citizen. When our child lives with a steady dose of positive support, we are doing our part to prevent society-wide behavioral problems.

I attended over eighteen hundred of my kids' games before they left our home. They are still talking about what that meant to them to have us arranging our world to support them. Blake just wrote this unsolicited note to me:

> *I've been thinking back over so much of what we appreciate. I wanted to tell you some of the things that I have been thinking about how much you mean to me as a son who is 27 now. I can't help but think back at the memories I have of a supportive mother who was always there for me, who did not know how to quit. No one ever taught you how to quit. I think you've instilled that in me too. I'm appreciative for it. And I think the other two bros got it from you too. But Mom, I always remember the old tennis matches where you'd always be out there. You put in your dues, Mom. You were always pickin' there. And I want to say thank you.*

Being a sports-mom was a season of life that is now changed, but the dividends continue to multiply.

Acceptance is felt through many avenues. Sitting through those years of Suzuki piano lessons and practices took work. Listening to my children talk about the things that hurt or intimidated them and showing empathy kept their hearts open and warm. Jean Lush believes listening is crucial. She says, "A mother who leads her children takes time to listen to their thoughts and feelings. She doesn't pretend to have all the answers, and she avoids jumping to conclusions. When her children ask for help, she is willing to assist them, but her goal is to help them learn, not to do everything for them."[8]

In 1994, *USA Today* reported that more than 1.6 million youngsters ages five to fourteen were left home alone each day from the time school dismissed until a parent returned.

> And the absence of supervision forces "these kids who are seriously looking for guidance or leadership, to go out and seek it on their own." George Meyer, a marriage and family therapist with Long Island's Institute of Psychoanalysis, says the group he worries about most are the 12-, 13-, and 14-year-olds. They are the most volatile group. Educational psychologist Linda Kreger says some parents think "the children are much more competent than they really are."[9]

A wise mom will continue to be aware of all that she can do to nurture. She will remember not to stop nurturing when the children are independent physically because she knows the unseen realms still need support. The opportunity to encourage beautiful fruit demonstrates God's design for femininity and how women were created to reflect a bright light.

## 6. Hovering over a completed process, honoring, participating with enthusiasm

### Nurturing Result –
### The child FEELS: loved, valued, emotionally prepared, safe

Hovering requires patience and perseverance. Those are character qualities directly stemming from the heart of God. With our long-range nurturing process, we are likely to experience some tribulation along the way. Romans 5:3–6 tells us how tribulation brings about perseverance, which brings about proven character, which brings about hope, which does not disappoint.

Take the advice of one of my favorite T-shirts: "THINK BIG." Don't just focus on some menial task or allow your selfish inclinations to tempt you to jump ship early. Rather, stay till quittin' time. Move up above the clouds occasionally to gain a clear perspective so you're confident with why you're going through all this. Just as stew on the stove needs to simmer a long time, children need long-term nurture. Stir the pot frequently, add a little water, and wait for the flavors to merge. Maybe the stew needs some spices, or perhaps some of the fat should be removed. Nurturing is the same. We make additions as we sense the need. When we make mistakes, we identify them and make adjustments.

One woman who wanted the best for her family wrote to me about how she thought she had been a responsible mother. Yet she was seeing too many of her own failures in her kids. Perhaps my written reply to this woman will be helpful.

> Dear _____,
>
> You said, "We feel we have failed them spiritually," and yet you said, "We never missed an event" and "we encouraged them in their lives." The truth is this:
>
> 1. You shouldn't be too hard on yourself. (We have all fallen short to some extent.)
> 2. Your physical expressions have been expressions of the reality of spiritual truths or principles:
>    • Sacrificing for your kids
>    • Being spontaneous to meet their needs
>    • Showing love by your actions toward your kids
> 3. You have modeled God's kind of love.
>
> In answer to your question, "What can I do now with so little time to salvage—What is your advice?" I would offer these suggestions of *action* to take.
>
> 1. *Thank* the Lord for the insights He's given you where you *have* shown God's love through your care, where you *have* done it right.
> 2. *Ask* the Lord to continually multiply your positive efforts.
> 3. *Work* at repeating the right things you've learned whenever possible.

4. *Remind* your kids of your love now—notes, calls, and honoring days or events important to them with hands-on displays of expression).

5. *Provide* pictures in frames for your kids of times that were positive and wonderfully meaningful. That way you'll multiply the memories.

6. *Ask* your kids for forgiveness where you've fallen short. Your humility will warm their hearts and provide a great model for them.

7. *Be available* when you know it will help or encourage them.

8. *Find* ways continually to show you're interested in completing the meeting of their needs.

9. *Tell* them of *your* renewed spiritual awakening and tell them you want to be available to encourage them in this same kind of development.

10. *Remember* that this is the first day of the rest of your life. Be happy and rejoice over your renewed *vision*.

You are a wise woman to be so perceptive in wanting to do all you can for your children. We are all continually growing and learning in the area of parenting. You are not alone. We're all in it together. Our responsibilities change but we never quit being a mom. Remember that God is on our side and will give us the wisdom and strength that we need. He desires our success as much or more than we do.

Warmly, Linda Weber

Is it worth it? You decide. Blessings on you as you make your investments in future security.

# The Opposite Side of Nurturing—
# Not Nurturing

Unfortunately, we human beings don't see ourselves clearly at times. Until we have spelled out what we are doing wrong, we often assume all is well. Even the Scripture starts its definition of what love means in 1 John 4:10 by saying what it is *not*. Each of the following six sections is the negative correlation to the already presented positive aspects of nurturing. May we learn by carefully spotting the potholes of life in which to avoid falling.

## 1. Hoping for the best, being distant, assuming all is well, actual abuse

*Result of NOT nurturing—*
*The child FEELS: trampled, overshadowed, overlooked, abandoned, uncared for, afraid, desperate, powerless, shamed*

If we have problems ourselves, we have no capacity or even desire to develop someone else. If we don't like or accept ourselves or if we are full of anger, we will generate more of the same. Our society is becoming more and more bankrupt of nurturing power. Even Dr. Spock, at age ninety-one, decided he had to write another book to help alleviate the situation.

> This one, he says, has nothing to do with the daily care and feeding of America's youth. *A Better World for Our Children*, published in 1994 by National Press, is about the educational, ethical, and spiritual poverty in which we are raising children and the awful legacy we are creating.
>
> Just ask and he'll reel off his list of atrocities: "Instability of marriage and the family; cruel competitiveness in business, sports and education; racial and ethnic divisiveness; materialism running rampant, with no spiritual or ethical values to offset it; increasing violence; lack of high-quality day care; an educational system that spews out children with no skills, no goals and no preparation for productive, satisfying lives.

"Tote it up," he says, "and you have a picture of a society speeding downhill."[10]

People may get a good laugh from the movie *Home Alone*, but some of the comments to and about the boy in the lead role display a large disregard for his need for nurturing, which is true for many children. Consider this comment from *Insight* magazine:

> Audiences can enjoy the comedy of home-alone kids when they are depicted in the movies, but parents have discovered that latchkey children are no laughing matter. Increasingly women—and men—realize that a loving parent is not only crucial in those early helpless years of babyhood, but teenagers who miss out on parental supervision after school find destructive ways to entertain themselves.[11]

How does it happen that we provide only shells for our children to live in? We tend to forget about invisible needs. When we overlook the emotional and spiritual needs of children, we introduce to the world a child with insecurity and inner hostility. By allowing the pressures of life and our own selfishness to overwhelm us and divert attention from nurturing, we erect a large backdrop for many negative dramas.

## 2. Discouraging children, offering no responsibilities/consequences, being too permissive or too domineering/controlling, abusing child's right to be nurtured

### Result of NOT nurturing –
### The child FEELS: *confused, wounded, insecure, emotionally scarred, betrayed, unstable*

Taking responsibility has become a lost art, and children who take responsibility are even harder to find. Blaming someone else for whatever happens is the trend. We plead, "I'm a *victim*."

"It can't be my fault. It isn't fair," we say. "I have a right to do what I want. I did my best and look what happened. You owe me. I'm being taken advantage of. Poor me. I don't deserve this. Nobody's considering me. Everybody else is wrong, and I'm right." A victim mentality is a display of selfishness that lacks any elements of nurturing. Nurturers take responsibility for their mistakes and their faults, and they train others to do the same.

Proverbs 29:18 says, "Where there is no vision, the people are unrestrained." When people live without consequences, bedlam rules. If we allow children to do whatever they want (be sloppy, be selfish, break the rules, be negligent, defend their wrong choices by claiming they are victims, ignore confrontation, talk back harshly, or generally get away with sin), we are promoting disasters.

In her book *Mothers and Sons,* Jean Lush speaks about the need for mothers to discipline and establish consequences for their sons, which is equally true with daughters.

> Indulgent mothers . . . not only let children do what they want, they also give them too much and make too many sacrifices for them. . . . They rarely make their children do anything around the house, but typically wait on them hand and foot. . . . If only the indulgent mother could realize her silver cords are too tight. She's teaching her son to be overly dependent and hindering his development in the process.
>
> One study reported that homosexual men had unusually close relationships with their mothers. They were babied through childhood. Their mothers were excessively affectionate and fostered an undue dependency in them. Because Mom was overprotective and indulgent, this made her much easier for the little boy to cope with than Dad. Her type of mothering seemed to whittle down the chances of the father being a strong male model to his son.
>
> Overdependence on Mom after the latency years is harmful. I've noticed that boys during junior high often act cruelly and hatefully toward their mothers. Periodically they are cold and distant.[12]

One of the most devastating traits a mom can have that will negatively affect her family is a domineering/controlling spirit. According to Peter and Barbara Wyden, "Another type of mother who is in charge of raising homosexual boys is the mother who dominates the family. In a study of 106 homosexuals, 81 had dominating mothers."[13] Lush agrees with the bad effects when "women [are] the chief authority figures in their homes. Children tend to identify most with whoever holds the most powerful position in their lives. All mothers, with or without husbands, can choose whether they will lead their children or dominate them. There is a difference. In most cases she is very organized and efficient in performing tasks, but she railroads people in the process."[14]

Whether you have sons or daughters, if your tendency is to control, please identify the problem and seek adequate help for the sake of all around you. Your kids' marriages and much more are at stake.

## 3. Too busy, tired, stressed, divided, and selfish to attend to heart needs, downing everything

### Result of NOT nurturing –
### The child FEELS: angry, rejected, resentful, indifferent

This one hits us all hard. Life is so busy. We never get everything accomplished on our to-do lists. And because we don't have "nurturing the children" on our list, we often fail to leave the margins we need to raise healthy children.

In the middle of meeting deadlines, outside expectations, and regular chores, it's easy to be distracted when our child comes with some seemingly insignificant request. They feel our ongoing disinterest.

Years ago I spent too much time on the phone counseling people through hard issues. My three-year-old son couldn't get my attention on a long-term basis, so he tried something drastic.

That little boy took off the knobs from the keyboard cover of our piano. The knobs were old, and the screws holding them in place were stripped and could be easily removed. Unfortunately, the ends of those exposed screws were sharp and did a lot of damage to the front panel of the piano as this son scraped them back and forth repeatedly.

When I saw what happened, you can believe he paid a price for his actions. But I also got the message that I was not tuned in to his heart. 'Twas a good lesson for Linda Weber years ago. Maybe it can be a reminder for you too.

This state of parental busyness and inattentiveness is fostering serious consequences. Consider these comments from an editorial in *USA Today:*

> Guns make the violence worse, but guns are not the cause. I believe part of the cause may be "benevolent" neglect. . . . Parents need to realize that kids need parental love, not TV, not computers nor paid strangers as baby-sitters. Beyond keeping our kids off the street, we need to keep them on the high road. Officials need to realize that when kids act out, they need attention. . . . This is not only a crime of violence, it is a crime of indifference.[15]

Do we know what we are doing when we show such indifference? My daughter-in-law Jami Lyn has seen the fruit of indifference in her high school classrooms. She knows the kids have what it takes intellectually to learn. Yet kids demand attention and want to be entertained. "Is the need to be entertained related to the television as baby-sitter," she asks, "or lack of conversation at home, especially at meal times?" Oh, that we could see how *our* indifference toward our children and our *kids'* indifference toward learning is connected.

## 4. Ignoring clues of deviance and pain, avoiding provision of wise counsel, neglecting emotional needs of the heart, allowing a silent destruction (like the frog boiling to death, one degree at a time)

### Result of NOT Nurturing –
*The child FEELS: unimportant, depressed, poorly about self, apathetic, destructive*

Can you pick up any clues from the following comments that point to a boy who just *might* have a serious problem that should not be ignored?

✔ "A boy with a dark side and an obsession with bombs and violence."

✔ "Students said he daydreamed about killing people as if they were in a video game."

✔ "He talked about guns and blowing up things all the time during class."

✔ "Kip said he was going to bring his guns to school, kill a few people and save one shot for himself."

✔ "On his Internet service account, Kinkel described his hobbies as 'role-playing' games, heavy metal music, violent cartoons/TV, sugared cereal, throwing rocks at cars and EC Comics."

✔ "For an occupation, he wrote: 'Student, surfing the Web for info on how to build bombs.'"

✔ "Kinkel openly displayed a dark side to his peers."

✔ "Kinkel listened to the music of self-described Satanist rocker Marilyn Manson, presented a three-minute talk in class on how to build a bomb and gave a friend a device to break into a car as a birthday present. . . . He illustrated it with a detailed picture he had drawn of an explosive connected to a clock."

✔ "Expressed a fascination with death and destruction to his peers long before he allegedly killed his parents and opened fire in a crowded school cafeteria."

✔ "In a literature class this semester at Thurston High School, when it was Kinkel's turn to share from his journal, he routinely stood in the front of the room and read about his plans to 'kill everybody.'"[16]

When these comments were printed about Kip Kinkel, one newspaper headline stated, "The Suspect: Most Adults Missed Warning Signs." Kip shot both his parents to death besides opening fire in a crowded cafeteria, killing two students, and wounding twenty-two, one dark day in May of 1998. What a stark example of needs that were visibly brewing, yet nobody stopped or stepped in to take preventive action.

## 5. Needing to be elsewhere, distant, demonstrating disapproval, unaware, sharing only the residence, children left with adult responsibilities, giving kids substitute love (things), alienating them

*Result of NOT nurturing—*
*The child FEELS: abandoned, haunted by emptiness,*
*disapproved of, rejected*

Dr. James Comer, a professor of child psychiatry at Yale Child Study Center, says this: "Vast numbers of children are growing up without any kind of good relationship with adults, making it almost impossible for society to stop them when they're violent."[17]

Good relationships in general have to start at home or our children won't know what to do later when trying to develop one. If your level of intimacy sees sharing as simply leaving notes for each other on the refrigerator and sleeping in the same house, you're going to experience the results of your child's hurt feelings.

Sometimes life demands more of us than we've planned. On our way to pick up *another* baby-sitter, we stop to buy some "thing" to give our child to pacify sad feelings. Giving things is an attempt to stop our guilt feelings too.

I'll never forget a conversation I overheard in a phone kiosk at the airport. A young executive mom called her three-year-old to tell the little girl about a toy she was dropping off between lengthy business trips. All the mother talked about with the little girl was this cool toy. Most of her phone time was spent giving the live-in nanny more instructions. As she hung up the phone, I could see this mother mentally saying, "Check, nurturing done." She had accomplished the required "mothering" and had moved on to the rest of her list.

# 6. Absentee parent can't see a child's dying heart (the child even needs to make an appointment with the parent simply to ask a question)

*Result of NOT nurturing—*
*The child FEELS: empty, sad, lonely, hopeless, isolated, explosive*

You've read biographical sketches in newspapers and magazines of people who have committed violent crimes. In every case, their upbringing lacked that close nurturing touch to help them feel accepted, important, and cared for. The infamous Oklahoma City bombing suspect, Timothy McVeigh, was noted in the media as having become depressed and a loner when his parents divorced.

When I have "needed" (chosen) to be away from my children, I wasn't able to contribute adequate input about anything, nor was I able to monitor their feelings about what was happening in their lives. I sensed negative trends developing. Because of that, I chose to minimize my time away.

Hurting children with absentee parents have no place to go with their pain and the void they feel. And the absentee parent has no touch with the child to channel the problems into a healing pattern. Hill Walker, director of the Institute for Violence and Destructive Behavior at the University of Oregon, says, "Young people are walking around like powder kegs waiting to explode. Anything—body language or a look—could ignite them."[18]

Do we just let them explode, or do we stop and change our lack-of-nurturing syndrome? Brenda Hunter speaks to this absence/presence issue in *The Power of Mother Love:*

> It's an illusion to think we can cheat our children of our love and presence now and make it up to them later. The season for child rearing is when our children are growing up in our homes before our very eyes. That's the time to give them hugs, kisses, and abundant time. That's the time to teach them values and deliver up to them our humanity. And if we elect to spend our valuable but fleeting time

142

otherwise? One mother said it well, "There are no second acts with children."[19]

# Conclusion

Feelings are real. Children are going to feel something—positive feelings or negative feelings. Before you retire from parenting, evaluate your nurturing style. Do you realize which route you are following?

Mothers make an incredible difference, one way or the other. I hope you realize your gifting and feel empowered to influence the lives around you. I pray that you will slowly meditate on the principles here to fully benefit your family's heritage. Because time is so important, one young mom who caught a glimpse of her value after reading *Mom, You're Incredible*[20] wrote this, "Thank you for helping me realize how important my role as a mother is before it is too late and my children are grown." My prayer is that your perspective is heightened and your hope is strong for all you can be as a nurturer! It is a big part of femininity. God bless you in your pilgrimage as a reflector of light!

## CHAPTER 10

# Letting Go – the Culmination

*T*he day after Ryan's high school graduation he moved across the mountain to live with his brother for the summer. Although I knew it was coming, I still wasn't ready. It happened so fast. I sat at my desk pondering the graduation festivities we all enjoyed, and tears started to flow. When Ry came back at the end of the summer, he would only be home long enough to pack and move to Wheaton College in Illinois. He wouldn't be living at home anymore, except for vacation visits. That didn't feel good. One summer he went to Africa, and then he got married right after college. It was over. Even though I saw it coming, it somehow felt like a shock when it happened.

It was hard when we drove away from Kent as he went off to college. Dad and I both shed a few tears. When it was time for Blake to leave, the same feelings filled our souls. With only Ryan left, he seemed like an only child. Things had always been busy at our house, like they are at yours. Then, suddenly, that twenty-five-year nurturing window slammed shut. My loss could not be put into words. I guess this is why I hear moms say, "I don't want to hear about it," when the subject surfaces. The end of my influential years of preparing my children for walking life's path had arrived. Why would any of us want something so wonderful to come to a screeching halt? What a tough assignment for our femininity.

# No More

There are no more boys, big or little. (I love my boys!) I can't ask them what they want for breakfast anymore. It's hard making and eating strawberry crepes without them. I think of those unique cakes I made for their birthdays—I'll make no more. The practice and game schedules to keep up with are no more. No more lists of phone messages. No more hosting the friends' stopovers. No more shirts to buy. No more, "What'cha got to eat, Mom?" (I've even gotten ambushed by an outburst of tears as I write this. This is one emotionally charged subject.)

I won't be filling double carts with groceries anymore. I'll not be buying seven gallons of milk at a time, and the gallon I have now will sour before we are able to finish it. I used to buy twenty loaves of bread at a time, and now one loaf gets moldy before we eat it. I won't be making double and triple batches of cookies because there's no one here to eat them. No more loud music. No more pleading to "Please clean up that room!" No more gas tanks on empty. No more requests for a five-dollar bill.

There are no more graduations (although, there are a few graduate-level parties left). Most everything is over. Even all our boys' weddings have come and gone, which is the true test of letting go. But . . . that's not the end. We have three daughters now, and they are wonderful. Jami Lyn, Jessica, and Carolyn are part of our family. There will be another season with grandchildren one of these days, and you can be sure that I anticipate this with much pleasure. Carol Kuykendall sums it up this way: "Though some grieving is normal, I knew I faced a choice: I could continue to wallow in nostalgia and dwell on the past—or embrace the future."[1] Says easy, does hard.

# Understanding Requires Education

Letting go doesn't come naturally. Christian leaders are quick to say that parental interference is at the top of the list for causing troubled marriages. It is a common problem. As the primary nurturer in the home, Mom needs an extra measure of encouragement. Drs. Cloud and Townsend have some helpful insights:

> The process of leaving mother emotionally is the final developmental step for the child, enabling him to make a full commitment to adulthood.
>
> The first separation from mother, a physical one, is called *weaning* in the Bible. The Hebrew word translated *wean* is a positive word that sometimes means "brought up" and "to deal bountifully, to reward, or to ripen." The child is taken off the breast when he has had enough of the good stuff of early dependency and is *ripe* for the next step.
>
> The second separation—leaving home—has been described as the wounding of mother, which every child eventually does. They abandon her, in the sense that they grow up and no longer *depend* on her as mother. This does not mean that they no longer love, adore, relate to, give to, or receive from mother. *The relationship is not over, but it is changing.* Mother is no longer *the* source.
>
> A mother takes great satisfaction in being her child's source. She is his first source of life and nurturance. And then his source of wisdom, discipline, friendship, teaching, values, and many other virtues. It is a very satisfying and rewarding role for Mom.
>
> The sad news for her is that the role is designed to end. She gives life, prepares her child for life, and then lets go of the life she has created.
>
> The "letting go," as we've seen, is the hard part for the mom. The child's task is to inflict the wound of leaving—

to "take" his life and run with it. The mother's role is to "take" the wound and contain it. She sheds the bittersweet tears of letting go and mourning the empty nest. She watches as an independent person emerges—the fruit of her nurture, discipline, and love. Joy and sadness are the combined themes of this wound. It is at once a happy and painful tearing away.

To the extent that a mother is able to allow this step to take place peacefully, things go well. She has to reclaim the values of separateness, difference, limits, and assume a stance against regression. . . . She should relish in this sad step, and that is a difficult thing to do. But as she does it, she can see the independence of her child not as a threat but actually as a symbol of her good work: He is now on his own.[2]

To sum this up, these doctors say,

The parent gradually turns over the management of the child to the child. The parental role disappears. The axiom is this: *To the extent that a person is being parented, to that extent this person is still a child.* The person who is an adult, yet acts like a child, will encounter problems when jobs and relationships require adult behavior.[3]

Did you ever wonder how it is that girls tend to stay closer to the original home front? "Girls are moving from someone feminine and warm to someone a little scary and intimidating. The problem is a little like a rocket leaving Earth's orbit. The little girl has more 'g's' keeping her close to Mother Earth. She must work harder than her brother at leaving that orbit in order to move into the outer world," Cloud and Townsend tell us.[4]

All this "leaving stuff" is part of God's design. It's part of being that jewel who is reflecting light. Ruth Myers helps us catch this concept. "I am one of Your spiritual masterpieces, created clean and clear as a flawless jewel . . . and that You are cutting and polishing me to receive and display more fully the beauty of Your glorious attributes!"[5] Letting go can be part of this beauty.

# Help Me Be Convinced

We experienced something a year ago that demonstrated this principle of letting go. The elders of our church decided to give Stu and me a special gift for twenty years of loyalty after starting Good Shepherd Community Church. They enlisted several master craftsmen within our church to design and create a dining room table—that extends to seat twenty) and ten lovely chairs for our new home.

David and Denny handpicked every piece of wood. The table and chairs were crafted over a long period of time. Utmost care was given to the handling of this superior Pennsylvania-cherry masterpiece. After laboring over it with love, David excitedly delivered it to us. I asked him, "How do you feel about parting with this, when it has become so much a part of you?"

Without hesitating, he spoke profoundly about the principle of letting go. "This has been designed and crafted for you. Its purpose is now being realized as you take and use it. I took pleasure preparing it for you, and I walk away with no regrets knowing the purpose is complete." Wow! I still get goose bumps. His words capture the heart of our mission to nurture—so we can let them go. God lets us in on raising His children. When His purpose is complete, we follow His wishes and let them go.

# Understanding with Analogies

There are so many pictures that help us identify with this act. For a woman, it is easy to think of the gestation period of the child she carries in her womb for nine months. The babe is protected with lining and fluid to aid in the safe development. It wouldn't be possible for the child to live or be without problems if he were born too soon. Timing is critical. At the end of nine months, for the mother to say, "I don't want this baby to be born yet; let's wait a few months" is absurd. But think. Do we try this with our children when it is time to let go?

What about the cut flowers we enjoy from the florist? They are picked when their beauty is at its peak. Holding them causes withering. Before they were picked, they, too, had to go through a long process of nurturing. If the gardener hadn't studied the needs, prepared the soil, fertilized, watered, pruned, and picked off the dead parts, the flower's full beauty wouldn't have materialized. The flowers also had to have proper sun exposure. The gardener got a lot of pleasure watching the beauty unfold one petal at a time and watching the variations bloom. If the gardener had been selfish and not cut the flower, no one else would have enjoyed its beauty.

We can't keep fruit on the tree, ships in port, letters in the box, arrows in the quiver, runners in the blocks, or students in school. There is a time to let go.

# Trying To Be Cerebral

You are probably saying, "Our hearts are breaking over this transition, and you're asking me to be cerebral?" You know I'm in the same condition, so let's hold each other's hands and do our best. There are some timeless truths in Genesis 2:24, Matthew 19:4–6, and Ephesians 5:31—namely, to leave and cleave.

Carol Kuykendall looks at the challenge: "Letting go is a God-given responsibility, as important as love in the parent-child relationship. Without it, children cannot grow. With it, they gain the confidence and independence to seek and reach their potential in life."[6] She also says this: "Our children will not give up their childish ways unless they sever their bonds of dependency upon us. They cannot grow up in every way unless we withdraw our control from their lives to allow them to mature independently. . . . We have to let go and give them the freedom to learn for themselves and to allow them to fulfill God's purpose for their lives—not ours."[7]

# Preparing for Healthy Independence

We start the process of nurturing healthy independence as soon as the child is born. The umbilical cord is cut, meaning that the child must now take an active role in gaining sustenance. The child learns to feed himself, walk by himself, and ride a bike. Can you imagine how tired you'd be if you never let go of that bicycle? Later we let him go off to school and spend the night at a friend's. We wonder if he can make it without us.

I remember the day Kent got his driver's license. Both Kent and Blake drove away that day for the first time. I wondered if I was ready for this. Was I foolish for letting both boys go together? Would they return alive? (Their memorable parting words that day were, "Hope to see you again.")

But the stakes get higher. They start dating and then go off to college. All these preliminaries lead up to the grand finale. It's like setting the stage for the drama with all the props in place. Are we ready to open the curtain for the act of independent living to begin?

Preparing for this stage requires good skills on the mother's part. Drs. Cloud and Townsend say,

> The good mother refuses to tie her children to the nest and instead kicks them out. By "nest" here, we mean dependent behavior past the time when that behavior is appropriate. The good mother then is internalized as a structure within the child against his own regressive wishes to be taken care of when what he needs is to grow up. Then in later life, when the person wants to bail out of adult responsibilities, a voice inside says no.[8]

Mom's personal insecurities can get in the way of the child developing a healthy independence. Drs. Cloud and Townsend provide this illustration: "Jeri's mom used guilt to control her. When Jeri would do or plan things that took her away from Mom, the message was clear: 'You are destroying me by being independent.' A child cannot cope with the fact that she is hurting her mother."[9]

# I Keep Wanting To Help

The first time we left the boys home while we were away on a speaking trip, I worried that they would not hear their alarms and get off to school on time. Should I call? I decided not to. Did they get up on time? No. Did they learn their lesson for the next time? Thank the Lord, yes.

Sometimes the best teacher is experiencing a "safe" failure. Carol Kuykendall adds this: "In the infant stage, we show our love by protecting them. As they mature, however, we must change the way in which we show our love to them. Slowly and gently we must give up this protection and control and allow them to protect and control themselves."[10]

# A Good Foundation Is the Best Preparation

Before we build our building, we'd better lay our foundation. That's a given. Equipping our children means preparing them to make the right kinds of decisions. To bring them to maturity means to make them ready, or ripe. Show them how to do things. Then watch while they try that thing. Teach them life skills. Talk about viewpoints they might encounter. Present scenarios of diverse situations so they are aware of consequences. Tell them what is important and why. Tell them what to expect so they are prepared. Teach them about the differences between men and women.

Leaving home after being fully prepared is like taking a final exam after having thoroughly studied. Because you have prepared, you can draw upon familiar facts. You have confidence to proceed because you are ready. It takes the tension away when you are equipped and enabled. Moms, we can enable our children to have the same confidence for independence. We feed their root systems. They know their roots are growing and strengthening. They believe they are prepared to live without us. And we know that *we* can live without them by our side.

Erma Bombeck expressed her thoughts about life without the kids: "My excuse for everything just got on that bus. . . . It's the end of an era. Now what do I do for the next twenty years of my life? These walls have been so safe. . . . I didn't have to prove anything to anyone. Now I feel vulnerable."[11]

# It Takes Love to Give Freedom

Our children will soar when we set them up for it. I can't help but think of the setter on a volleyball team who puts that ball in the air, positioned for the spike. If the setter doesn't place that ball accurately, there can be no spike. The setter is the key player scouted by universities. You are the setter. You are needed by your son or daughter to set them up in life. Maybe it doesn't feel good to have done so much "prework" only to hand them over to their marriage partner. But that is the whole goal of the setter—to make the set for the winning spike.

Freedom not to live up to your expectations but for them to take off after "the set" is a gift of love. Ingrid Trobisch says it this way:

> Watch over your daughter in prayer, then let her go. One daughter may be more difficult to release than another. You, as a mature woman, know that when your beautiful child steps out to make dreams come true, the stars in her eyes won't solve all the problems that arise. Still, you let go because ultimately, you respect her. You love her enough to allow her to make her own mistakes, walk her own pathway, follow her own timetable.
>
> Because you respect yourself, you allow your daughter the freedom to not live up to your expectations. This is the best gift of all.[12]

# Evaluate Our Release Skills

"I mean well, but . . ." A mother "has the power to send one of two messages: 'Your individuality is loved,' or 'Your individuality is my enemy, and I will destroy it.' A child cannot stand up to that kind of attack and develop in the way that she needs to."[13]

Sometimes we need to evaluate our release skills. We need to ask ourselves if we would like done to us what we are doing to our children or inlaws. If your perspective is fuzzy, stand back and think things through. To participate in your child's healthy marriage will require your seeing a need for your own separateness. As you gain this wisdom, you enable your child to gain the perspective he or she needs to develop a strong bond with a spouse.

James Osterhaus has these tips:

> Healthy couples are composed of people who have left their families of origin. We've all heard the verse in Genesis 3 about leaving parents and cleaving to one's spouse. Jesus reiterated this point. Why is this important? "Leaving" is an emotional separation, not so much a physical one. When I'm too close to something or someone I can't maintain my perspective or see from different angles. I will tend to center on particular flaws or assets without seeing the whole picture. As I get distance, my perspective changes. I learn to see my parents for the good and bad they did in my life.
>
> My separateness allows me then to enter into a close bond with another. The paradox of a healthy marriage is that two separate, well defined individuals can enter into a bond much more closely and fully, while still maintaining their individuality.[14]

One friend told me of her experience with her mother-in-law, which is so common, unfortunately. Her mother-in-law is "in their face" constantly. She questions the way they spend money, wonders why my friend does this and that, and intimidates them about their decisions. She undermines their dreams and goals and insists on being in the middle of everything. Calling continuously, this mom won't let them establish a life of their own. You can imagine what holiday seasons are like when Mom is not happy. (Are we having fun yet?) My friend summed up her feelings by saying that she wished her mother-in-law would "stay out."

Ephesians 4:1–3 is a good passage about release skills: "Walk in a manner worthy of the calling with which you have been called, with all humility and gentleness, with patience, showing forbearance to one another in love, being diligent to preserve the unity of the Spirit in the bond of peace."

# Build for the Future

Picture getting your child ready for a honeymoon canoe trip. You actually carved this craft as a gift for your child and his or her spouse. You have labored over this canoe for years. You chose the best wood and designed quality throughout. You have even helped your child ahead of time to understand the principles of balance necessary to avoid capsizing. Before they leave, you check for leaks. The new spouse is already in the canoe and waiting to embark upon the journey. Your child puts one foot in, but then can't follow through with the other.

What's the problem? You won't let go of your child's hand. With one foot in that canoe, there's no way that child can comfortably put the other foot in, much less paddle away and feel good about being with this new mate. Because they are literally being held back, the couple can't give themselves away to their new mate for this trip. Every effort to take off is impossible because there's no freedom from the giver. Despite all your wonderful preparation, they become discouraged. If you continue to hold on to your child, this new couple can't embark upon this well-planned trip. Frustration levels remain high, as the couple feels pressure to quit.

Moms, we want to help them off, don't we? We want to encourage them to feel good about building a strong marital union. We want to support the right decisions that develop healthy independence. We want to enable them to cling to each other and not feel gripped by our control. It's a tough scene when the "child's" attitudes and actions are held hostage by the emotional grip of a mom's insecurity. The generations ahead lose unless we choose to build for the future.

# Wholeness out of Brokenness

Ingrid Trobisch says, "Wholeness out of brokenness means rediscovery of simple pleasures."[15] She goes on to speak of such pleasures as wind, rain, snowflakes, a hug, and the skin of a baby. "It is also letting go of places and people you cherish in order to move on. It is sifting through the important and separating the good from the essential. Wholeness out of brokenness means hard decisions and difficult tasks that only grief-work can help you finish. . . . Wholeness comes in affirming everything and every place I have been as well as what lies ahead."[16] A friend even told Trobisch that she had now said "yes to her femininity."[17]

When we come to the point where we can give the next generation freedom to grow on their own, we set them up to possess the security they need. Paradoxically, after we've granted their freedom, they feel more ready to include us back into their lives. That is experiencing wholeness out of brokenness.

# Axioms to Affect our Decisions

Matthew 6:24 says, "No one can serve two masters; for either he will hate the one and love the other, or he will hold to one and despise the other. You cannot serve God and mammon." Somehow when our children become adults and often marry, we hang on to being in charge. We can discern some positive principles to live out through this advice from Drs. Cloud and Townsend:

> No matter how many miles apart and years distant you are from home, if you are still going to Mom for things you should be providing for yourself, you will always be a prisoner to your relationship with her—and that's not Mom's fault. . . . You might fight her 'control' or, you might try not to upset her. . . . You will be constantly reacting to your dependency on her, rather than living life deliberately, autonomously, and according to your own values and directions. . . . Remember that we can't separate from anyone in a vacuum. If Mom is still the only one residing within your heart of hearts—the one you still truly depend on—you won't be able to tolerate the tearing and isolation that will occur when you attempt to leave.[18]

# The Ultimate Act: Letting Go

The ultimate act of nurturing is letting go, allowing our precious children the freedom to experience the world on their own. We give them breathing room. As I was writing this chapter, I happened to be at the beach home of a friend who had purchased an exotic plant. When Donna took the plant to the house, she forgot to remove the plastic that was wrapped tightly around the pot. She watered it carefully, but because of the plastic the plant couldn't breathe. It was so saturated with water that it was "drowning and smothering," all at once. The beautiful flowers turned brown, and many leaves fell off. Death seemed certain.

After removing the plastic and letting the poor thing dry out, I removed the dead leaves and flowers. New leaves sprouted. It was exciting to see that there was still some life left. It looked like it was going to make it. Had that plastic not come off, there would have been no hope. Donna came close to losing her plant because she hung on to a piece of plastic. This is a picture of the "letting go" principle.

When Mom takes off that stifling emotional plastic, she gives her child the space he needs. The child gets to experience renewed health. If Mom didn't take off the plastic, she would eventually "suffocate" or emotionally harm her child.

When Blake was about to be married, I knew I had to give him wholeheartedly to his new wife. I needed her to know that she was to be the number one lady in his life and that I was relinquishing my "rights." I decided to write a poem, called *Apron Strings*, expressing my heart and making a public declaration of this new commitment. As I sat down to write, the tears flowed and I couldn't get past the first few lines. It took me three months to write that poem because it was so emotionally charged. I read it to Jami Lyn the night of their rehearsal dinner in the presence of all eighty-two guests. Most all present joined me with a tear or two.

The tears still flowed as I expressed the same kinds of things again when I gave Ryan away, in Apron Strings #2, written for Jessica. This was no small experience for me. (Both poems can be read in the introduction of *Mom, You're Incredible*.)

You would think that I had become accustomed to this trauma by the time I did it the third time, but no, I was still filled with incredible emotion. Apron Strings #3 went to Carolyn, wife of my oldest son, Kent, and is in the dedication of this book.

As you read the poem, I trust that you will think about your own mixed blessing of nurturing and launching. As hard as it is to do, the fruit is so good. What you end up passing down is a legacy from your life. As you own these truths, you'll agree with Erma Bombeck, that despite her fame and fortune, you, too, can maintain that "my legacy is going to be my three kids."[19] Blessings on you as you encourage them away from your wonderfully prepared nest.

PART 4

# Facet #3

# Relater Meant to Connect

## CHAPTER 11

# The Relational Genius

$\mathcal{P}$icture yourself at lunch with several girlfriends and each of you is talking excitedly. You are having so much fun catching up with each other. The conversations flit from subject to subject and back again. You rarely stay on one subject long enough to finish the story. When you go home that day and think about the conversations, you realize you don't know the endings of many of the stories. But you don't care because the purpose for being together was to enjoy your relationships.

I can just hear my husband if he overheard such a group. He would not appreciate the frenzy. Because he is a man, and different by definition, I know in advance that our responses in life are not the same. It's his nature to want to get to the bottom line and fix something—now. I want to circle the airport; he wants to land the airplane. He concentrates on solutions. I enjoy the warmth of relationships and simply want to enjoy the interactions as I talk about "whatever" with my friends. What matters to women is the interconnectedness of relationships. Anastasia Toufexis captures this thought:

> Relationship colors every aspect of a woman's life. . . .
> Women use conversation to expand and understand rela-
> tionships; men use talk to convey solutions, thereby end-
> ing conversations. Women tend to see people as mutually
> dependent; men view them as self-reliant. Women empha-
> size caring; men value freedom. Women consider actions
> within a context, linking one to the next; men tend to
> regard events as isolated.[1]

## There's Reason Behind It All

When we remember that God created our brains differently, we don't get so upset when the differences surface. We give each other more room to be different. Woman simply has better verbal and communication skills and is more sensitive and context-oriented because of her brain development.[2]

Women are better able to perceive and respond to multiple stimuli than are men. While the woman circles the airport in her plane, she may discover the nearest restaurant, locate the rental car building, and point out a landmark to her passengers. She is highly developed to circle that airplane. This is also why she is more emotional, more relational, and more sensitive. Because women are born with an exceptional verbal ability, it is easy to understand the facts that a Harvard study provides—that women speak an average of twenty-five thousand words per day as opposed to man's ten to twelve thousand words per day. It also helps explain why the woman has more words to speak at the end of the day when it seems her husband must have used his quota, as the joke would have it.

Study of the human body helps us understand why women can cross over and use the other side of the brain as well. "The corpus callosum is a thick bundle of nerves connecting the brain's right and left hemispheres. It is often wider in the brains of women than in those of men. It may allow for greater cross talk between the hemispheres—possibly the basis for woman's intuition."[3] Because of their brain's interconnectedness, women are able to work with multiple tasks simultaneously. Also, "more women listen equally with both ears while men favor the right one."[4]

There's something to female intuition. *Time* magazine tells us that women possess an ability to read other people's motives and meanings to some degree.

When shown pictures of actors portraying various feelings, women outscore men in identifying the correct emotion. They also surpass men in determining the emotional content of taped conversations in which the words have been garbled . . . women [have] greater skill in interpreting the cues of toddlers before they are able to speak.[5]

Intuition and empathy both relate to woman's wide awareness:

> Women, much more than men, tend to empathize with a friend who is hurting. A study of 15,000 women by *Family Circle* magazine found that 69 percent would rather talk to their best friend than to their spouse when they are feeling unhappy. Part of this is because another woman can uniquely understand many of a woman's life circumstances.[6]

Cloud and Townsend say this ability to empathize . . .

> brings its own special problems. Women are more connectors at heart than are men. They have more constitutional strengths in bonding, just as men do in aggressiveness. Being a "lover, not a fighter" . . . you feel the pain of others. You sense the depth of others' struggles, and you know what they need. It is a primary prerequisite for any meaningful relationship. Women have wonderful abilities to be empathic.[7]

# Relational Connection in Process

Stu and I were watching a young girl's basketball game a few years ago. The players were new at the game and hadn't scored any points for some time. Finally, when the first ball went through the hoop, they gathered in the middle of the floor to hug and celebrate their accomplishment. They were relationally expressive. Meanwhile, the other team took the ball down the floor unnoticed and scored two points. It was more important to the first team to relate to each other than to defend some basketball hoop.

About a year ago, I decided to have a "big girls" slumber party at my house. Because women are often getting others ready to go have fun, I decided that the older girls needed a night out to just enjoy relating. The fifty women who came couldn't stop speaking about how much fun it was to simply talk all night. I figured our group "share time" would take an hour and a half. Five hours later, we were still going strong. They loved the opportunity to do what they do so well—get next to others and bask in the warmth of relating.

Regardless of differences in women, the need to connect is there. A young single mother of three comes to my house to assist me. One day she told me she knows what it is like to be needy from her days as a child and now with children of her own. Although Consuelo has little, she sends money every month to a world organization to help sponsor a young child. Consuelo has a heart that wants to connect with the needy. This relational genius fulfills the verse in Proverbs 31:20: "She extends her hand to the poor; / And she stretches out her hands to the needy." Bless her.

# A Pattern after the Living God

God the Father says, "'As one whom his mother comforts, so I will comfort you'" (Isa. 66:13). He demonstrates relational strength. God the Son was the ultimate connector through His death and resurrection so that a holy God in heaven and sinful humanity could be connected. His sacrifice for us is our example of how we can ultimately relate to others in meaningful and profound ways.

It is God the Holy Spirit who comes alongside as the Paraclete. A woman is designed to function much like this relational example. As mankind is born of woman, we are "born of the Spirit" when we choose to follow Him (see John 3:5–6, 8). The Spirit comes alongside to help, to encourage, to console, and to comfort. The Spirit bore us, shares His divine life, sustains, teaches, helps, guides, and consoles. We have the same inborn abilities to be the relational genius in following this pattern. Just as the Spirit abides with us (is *with* us forever, John 14:16–17), He says, "I will not leave you as orphans; I will come to you" (John 14:18).

# Connecting with Man

Since men and women are so different, how can we connect? Because men are analytical and factual in their thinking, we need to speak their language. Because we are more abstract in our thinking, we need to convert our thoughts to be able to express feelings. We can help men by using word pictures when we explain our feelings to them and when they try to communicate to us. When I told Stu what my arm felt like before I had carpal tunnel surgery, I compared it to a bicycle's chain coming off and missing its connection. I expressed my pain by using something that he knew and understood.

During times when we feel "low" from a lack of emotional connection, we might say that we feel like a house that needs a paint job and some maintenance. The weeds need to be pulled, the roof needs to be replaced, and a few windows are cracked. We might add that when people walk by they don't notice our state of disrepair and that makes our house even more prone to decay. If we feel our husband is shutting us out, we might say we feel like we are inside a house. Some of the interior doors are locked, and we badly need to use those locked rooms. Without our attempts to paint a picture, our men might believe that everything is great. He may be thinking the goals have been accomplished—after all, he married you. Do make sure to provide lots of positive pictures as well.

Men don't have the crossover ability in the brain that women do. As much as we might try to nudge our husbands into thinking like we do, it can't happen. God made us differently. Our ability to process multiple facts simultaneously equips us with radarlike consciousness. We can't assume that men are like we are, because they are not. Even *Time* magazine placed a section of their lead article about differences between men and women in all capital letters: "HE CAN READ A MAP BLINDFOLDED, BUT CAN HE FIND HIS SOCKS?"[8] Our ability to relate and/or find things is simply more highly developed. It's literally "a brain thing."

Communicating through the use of the senses is important. We will be true relational geniuses when we fill the house with pleasant aromas of food when our husband is hungry. We will also feed him before we talk about deep significant subjects. Smelling good food and feeling full sets up both of you for a pleasant interaction. Such sensitivity speaks of knowing and responding to his needs. We can continue to meet those needs as we find practical ways to communicate through touch, sight, and hearing as well. This will increase our genius status.

We've been speaking of relating to our mate. These principles can also be used with friends, family, coworkers, and others. Learning to read people and be sensitive to needs is a gift we can continue to cultivate!

# What about My Feelings?

Having feelings is a big part of a woman's definition. God created feelings knowing women needed them to be the relational geniuses He planned. Men are different. Men are designed to be out there thinking globally, making decisions, and adding 2 + 2 to get 4 (using strong leadership with tough exteriors to forge ahead). Men often don't understand what a woman is "hung up on" when she is "back there" "feeling something." And women misconstrue why he seems so abrasive when he makes a decision without feeling anything.

We must never deny the part of us that God created. It is dysfunctional not to allow feelings or tears. Feelings are real. They express a sensitive heart that is saying, "Pay close attention." A woman cries tears of exuberance, joy, pain, and sorrow. Whether she has won an award, been surprised by friends, warmed by a gift, honored in a special way, or experienced the birth of a child, she feels strongly. And with the feelings in emotion, tears often flow.

Ingrid Trobisch quotes Edith Schaeffer with wisdom about our tears:

> Don't abort your afflictions. In other words, we do well to embrace the pain until its work is done. The human spirit in adversity can be a wondrous thing. Allow tears to flow. Scientists tell us they wash toxic chemicals from our bodies. Psychologists say they wash pain out of our hearts. Tears are the price we pay for loving. Unless grief-work is done, a person is kept from being fully alive. . . . Crying buckets of tears is a journey. It takes us from where we were before loss to where we'll be once we've adapted to the changes loss brings. No one can measure when those days are over. It requires patience with ourselves and with those who insinuate we should hurry up and get over it.[9]

Trobisch tells an African proverb from her long history of living in that country: "A lady never hurries." She speaks of uncluttering what is around and inside you and taking time to pick through the rubble of the explosions in your heart.[10] Who knows what causes all the tears to flow? But while we are crying, we have the Scriptures, which are full of reminders that our God knows and understands. (See Ps. 145:8–9, 18.)

# Relationship Drives a Woman's Being

Woman is so connected to those in her world that relationships with them are what drive her being. And those connections form her feelings. A woman's heart cries out for her needs to be met through her connected relationships.

A man is different. His importance comes through his work, his accomplishments, through conquering and solving life's issues. His concentration ability centers on tasks, not on relationships. (Isn't it interesting how God made us so different in order to complete one another?)

"When men try to kill themselves, it is commonly out of an injured sense of pride or competence, often related to work. When women attempt suicide, it is usually because of failures involving lovers, family, or friends."[11]

# Relational Skills Touch Home

There's more to relational skills than one might think. They enable woman to connect details in a home to create feelings. Terry Willits makes astute observations:

> Indeed, relationships affect the home atmosphere; but, the atmosphere we create in our homes can equally affect the relationships. . . . Are you frustrated by a husband or children or even friends who never seem to hang around home for long? Think about your home. Is it alluring and desirable? If your family's needs for love, pleasure, and security are not being satisfied in your home, they are much more likely to be tempted to find it somewhere else, somewhere that God never intended.[12]

Once again, our God-given powers enable us to provide for necessary connections that will affect all of history. The relational geniuses that we are comes across in how we create those essential settings in our homes. What a genius God created, and we can thank Him for allowing us to participate in His plan.

# Watch for Hazards—There's a Down Side

Being relationally blessed is a gift. Yet like most anything, there is a flip side to be aware of. In Proverbs, the Lord warns us about exercising this strength negatively. We see over and over how the devil can influence the woman in her relationships. She's relating all right—by connecting via flattery with her words; leaving the companion of her youth; having a smooth tongue as an adulteress; catching the man with her eyelids; dressing as a harlot; being cunning of heart, boisterous, and rebellious with feet not remaining at home; lurking by every corner; coming to seize and kiss a man (who is not her husband) and preparing her bed for him, enticing him, and seducing him. She even claims, "I have done no wrong." There are more references in Proverbs warning against this type of woman than exhorting about good relational qualities. (See endnotes for Scripture references to the above descriptions.[13]) Proverbs 7 also describes how she enticed the man through the senses—by sight, touch, smell, taste, and hearing.

There are also repeated references in Proverbs to warnings about women relating with a spirit of contention. The dictionary captures the essence of this concept we should avoid. We don't want to relate as a contentious woman—one who disputes and is aggressive, offensive, hostile, belligerent, quarrelsome, or polemical. (See endnotes for references of avoiding being contentious.[14])

Another negative relational hazard is addressed in Titus 2:3 regarding women in particular. We are not to be "malicious gossips." (See James 3:5–10 for a discussion about the tongue.) With a wavering tongue, we destroy, and yet we build too. With our tremendous capability to be verbal, we must be careful to let it keep our light shining through this blessed facet of femininity.

# Capitalize on Your Strength

On the positive side, Proverbs also speaks of relating with graciousness. A woman actually attains honor (Prov. 11:16). This covers the realm of body language and basically all forms of relating. We are to be showing discretion as we relate. When we don't, a nasty picture is portrayed in Proverbs 11:22; we are then "as a ring of gold in a swine's snout." When making wise choices in relating, Proverbs 31:26 says this of the woman: "She opens her mouth in wisdom, / And the teaching of kindness is on her tongue." She's aware of good timing. (Eccles. 3:7 says, "A time to be silent, and a time to speak.") Her tongue is soothing, is seasoned, is like a fountain of life, brings healing, guards her soul, and her words spoken in right circumstances are like apples of gold. And she is wise because she restrains her lips.[15]

A relational genius—what a privilege the living God has enabled us to be. May our connections enhance His reputation and reflect the light that He intends to shine through us.

C H A P T E R   1 2

# Importance of Being a Hub

*W*hen you picture the spokes of a wheel, do you think about the hub that safely holds all of the spokes together? Probably not. While everything runs smoothly and nothing squeaks, we take the wheel and its parts for granted, until something breaks down. Hobbling along or rendered completely immobile, we suddenly have a keen interest in fixing the broken part. We turn our attention to bringing the parts of the wheel back into harmony.

So it is in our relationships—whether at home, at the office, or in another group setting. When there are deadlines pressing, appointments pending, pressures mounting, and demands shouting, what will be the glue to keep the group together?

# The Connector

A woman's incredible relational abilities help her to be the hub that holds things together. How could we ever get the idea that we might be too important to be a hub?

If you look at a group that wants to accomplish a task or plan an event, you'll likely find a woman (or women) at the hub of it all, won't you? She pulls the pieces from every direction and has full command of all the little parts that must come together as she organizes and delegates. Because the hub is functioning so well, all the outlying factors "fall into place." She, the hub, makes it happen. You could say she is the glue that holds it all together.

I once asked Ryan how he would have felt had I worked full-time. Without a pause he said, "It would have been like we weren't a family. Everybody would have slept here, but I wouldn't have liked that. We've needed you to bind us together." He knew what he felt. Although he didn't call it a hub, that is what he meant. Mom was the person who brought everybody and everything together—great and small. Things ran smoothly because the hub was functioning. The individual parts were energized to pursue their own progress. All the spokes of our wheel were brought together to function as a strong unit. Looking back on my time at home with the children, I see even more clearly how important my job as the hub was. I ensured a connection within our family that no salary could ever compensate.

One mother who has crafted her own business so she can make her own hours and decline work that will take away her energy to be a hub said this: "I don't make my family, but I make everyone in it better. Because I am behind, supporting them, I give them the ability to be the best they can be."

Every woman does not have the luxury of arranging her own employment with flexible hours. I understand the frustration some women face as they strive to do their best in making adequate connections amidst challenging circumstances. These women reach deeply into their creative abilities and seek God's special wisdom for His kind of discernment. My own mother, raising us alone, turned away job offers in order to take jobs which allowed her the flexibility to come and go as needed. She could've made more money, but instead she made the choices that would care for us the best. She and many other women strive to be all they can by believing the words of the song, "God will make a way when there seems to be no way."

# Pictures of Your Hub Activity

Imagine what it would be like around a busy, international airport if they had no hub—no air traffic controllers keeping those planes on course.

Those of us who have played in bands or orchestras or sung in choirs know the value of a skillful director—a hub, if you will. The leader keeps everybody together in the same rhythm, and helps them end each section succinctly.

As our new home was being built, our building contractor had to pull together the right subcontractors at the appropriate time. If the painter had arrived the same day as the carpet layers and the framers, chaos would have resulted. The subcontractors would have been furious with the contractor. Had the contractor lost track of our project and forgotten to send even one contractor, say the electrician, our house would have lost its quality.

You are a hub. You are a connector. You possess abilities and antenna to reach out and bring everything together. The importance you bring to your family or life setting is beyond financial remuneration. Your powers as a master connector can make or break each person in your reach. Talk about influence! You've got it if you want it. (See appendices B, C, and D for various ways you function as a hub in the home, with children, and in an office/life setting.)

God knew what He was doing when He created woman as a relational being. All our in-born sensitivities to follow "our hunches" enable us to follow a trail when we see signs of insecurity and frustration. We can prevent trouble spots from exploding because we sense the need and help.

Our "electrical" power to connect with those around us is directly related to our spiritual energy source. The Bible tells us, "Those who seek the LORD understand all things" (Prov. 28:5). The more wisdom, insight, and discernment we gain from abiding with Christ, the stronger our power will be to connect. We can increase our connection strength by acquiring a greater reservoir of God's truth and then passing it on to others, just as a muscle gets stronger with use. Our effectiveness will be in direct proportion to the connection we have with the Father. He empowers us, like appliances are powered through being plugged into the socket. God directs us like an air traffic controller. He coordinates needs and schedules extra practice sessions like an orchestra director. But it is up to us to follow through as we, in His image, become the hub in our own sphere.

# Changing Society

If we maximize this concept of hub connection, we can change the world. We aren't directing airplanes to safety. Our work is even more important. We are promoting the stability and well-being of our precious families. We are protecting and directing hearts and spirits—psychologically, emotionally, and spiritually. Connection breeds feelings that will affect our family's behavior now and forever. Our connectedness saves their lives much turmoil.

Unfortunately, many assume that the "air traffic controlling" needed in their families will just happen. In a home or in any life situation, it is hard to predict which need will surface next.

There might be a physical need. I made many unplanned trips to the emergency room because of cuts, broken bones, allergic reactions, and other urgent, physical demands. There were mental needs too. Whether the boys needed books for a school project or answers to unending questions, they wanted someone to help them. They needed to learn how to break large assignments into smaller manageable tasks. They needed to learn how to memorize many facts or how to think through problems. Moms possess the privilege of channeling young thought patterns in the directions that would be most wise.

Of course, there were always emotional needs. Just having their caring mom there meant a lot. The things we constantly do to send mental and emotional messages of importance, acceptance, and care provide lifesaving opportunities that "buy" lifetime rewards. Active nurturing skills make being the hub of our home incredibly valuable.

# The Kitchen Connection

Stu and I have become seasoned air travelers. Many times I have seen those maps that show the air routes from city to city. Each airline has its own hub locations. United Airlines has hubs in Denver, Chicago, and Washington, D.C. The airlines operate most efficiently by using hubs. Our homes are the same way. When we think of the room in our house that is a hub, which is it? The kitchen, of course, attracts family and guests alike. Hearts are warmed as they get their tummies refueled.

Does that just happen? We who run the kitchen know that there is much planning, shopping, preparing, and inviting (not to mention cleaning) required before those wonderful dinnertime conversations can take place. We prepare a place, like Jesus did for us. The foresight that we possess and demonstrate allows our home to operate efficiently as a common ground for family and friends to connect at deep levels.

We've had fourteen hundred people through our home this last year or so. It has been fun but lots of work. Good relationships have been built. I see purpose to it all. And it feels good to observe the fruit that has been born and to realize that my hub work is so critical. We can't underestimate the value of our efforts.

# Hub Work Brings Joy

I will never forget what Chuck Swindoll told Kent's graduating class at Wheaton College. He reminded them, among all their future endeavors, that "it would be hardest at home."[1] Sometimes it's so easy to give our best to others and not to save energy for our families. But if we do, we will miss out on the opportunity to strengthen our home.

Do you find that it is hardest at home? Do you resent when others need you to pull the bits of their lives together? It is sometimes hard for us to enjoy home life, especially if our focus is elsewhere. Maybe God is calling us to find contentment where He's placed us. Relax and try to enjoy making others' lives sweeter. Terry Willits says, "The extent to which we enjoy our home life greatly influences how we enjoy the world. There is no greater way to fill our homes and hearts with life and love than by awakening our wonderful, God-given senses."[2] Enjoying our opportunities at home most likely will require understanding how all this happens.

## Always on Alert

One afternoon, one of our boys got a call from the soccer coach asking him to play tennis. Fortunately, I was home and able to assess the situation. Call it a mother's intuition or whatever, I felt uncomfortable with the request. I had no specific reason to be so upset but "something told me" to be concerned. My son did not understand my dismay, but he listened carefully. To make a long story short, the coach was later charged with being a sex offender with boys and, of course, was fired from his coaching job.

I'm so glad I was the hub to reject that connection. How valuable a hub can be, to "happen to be there" at unplanned moments to protect against trouble that may be lurking.

We have the option to choose to be involved in our children's lives and to run prevention programs at home for all the "stuff" we see happening around us. Remember, Mark 8:36 says, "For what does it profit a man to gain the whole world, and forfeit his soul?" I say, What good does it do to be tuned into all kinds of good and profitable things and yet ignore and maybe lose connection with your own kids? That is a question every mom must ask herself. Her answer must be balanced against the other question: What is it going to require?

## Little Things

Consider this from Ingrid Trobisch:

> Sometimes we don't see meaning in the little things and
> we are not conscious of how it all works together to create

a powerful image. The little things we do at home, like putting wildflowers in a vase, are invisible medicine for all the bumps and bruises of family life. The connections we make in our daily rounds, an old photograph tucked into a frame, a lullaby each evening by the bedside, a hug among fresh clean linens, are the putty that holds the mosaic together. Someday we will see the entire picture in the lives that come after us. Years of keeping the springs of the heart will at last be made visible.[3]

Our families need the connection we provide to keep the many pieces together. That connection passes beyond the physical realm into the unseen territory of the emotional and spiritual. The connections we are making are more than meets the eye.

## Your Attentive Presence Is Essential

You've seen those plate spinners on TV? They keep moving from plate to plate to keep those "hummers" going. Many times we women feel like plate spinners in life. We keep track of lots of schedules and keep everybody going to the next event. We arrange the transportation and make the next connection. Yet if we were not relating to everybody's needs along the way and helping them plug in where they are expected, needed, or wanted, things could fall apart. There must be a hub of connection, or disorientation will follow.

This central person helps decipher what is best for everyone along the way. Her relational skills tune her antennas to needs or dangers. With her incredible ability to make connections, she plugs everybody in just where they fit best. Many times they enjoy the fruit of everything "just falling together." And yet behind the scenes was the incredible woman at the hub, who foresaw it all and made it happen, edifying each person. She enacts the wisdom from 1 Corinthians 10:23, "All things are lawful, but not all things are profitable. All things are lawful, but not all things edify." This modern-day hub fulfills Scripture in practical ways every day.

176

# Hubs Make a Difference

I love watching God mightily use my husband. I have generally been the hub of connection in our home over the years. I kept a lot of pieces together while having a low profile. I admit that I get "antsy" at times, feeling I could be "accomplishing more out there." But the rewards now are great with the family God has given us. And I believe that so much of the secret, if there is a secret, lies in a woman's being a strong, steady hub unselfishly positioned to meet needs on every level.

None of us is perfect, but God has been good. On various occasions I have had men and women express their realization that my husband's ministry wouldn't be as effective if I wasn't fulfilling my role. Those comments always make me feel good. One time after I spoke about a woman's worth, a man told me he felt badly because he had not realized how valuable his wife was to their home. May his kind continue to be ignited with renewed appreciation for the women in their lives.

Plenty of times I have indulged in pity parties about being everybody's "go-fer." Yes, I could have made some different decisions along the way to spread out the responsibilities. But I wouldn't trade the stable family I have today for anything. We are not perfect, but as I always told the boys, "I'm thankful for the good things that I've got."

# You'll Have Season Changes

Seasons of life dictate much of what we do. "There is an appointed time for everything. And there is a time for every event under heaven" (Eccles. 3:1). My last cub left for college about the time I was working on my first book. My season of life had shifted, and I experienced the opportunity to venture out to another mission—to write *Mom, You're Incredible*. Earlier when I thought about writing, I remember thinking that I would never be able to do this consuming work and still be a tuned-in mom. Something would suffer. But now the season was different.

I definitely realize that I'm experiencing a different season of life. I wouldn't trade my former season of being a hub with the children at home—the rewards are very gratifying. And for now, I am thoroughly enjoying my present season. Each one of us has different circumstances, but the challenge is to complete our God-given mission to honor Him most during each season of life. I may not have children at home anymore, but I still experience being a hub of connection by establishing and maintaining extended-family relationships. You can be a hub in whatever situation of life in which you find yourself as well.

Even single women can find ways to be hubs. In their book for single women, Joy Jacobs and Deborah Strubel discuss the benefit of finding a ministry area: "One of life's paradoxes is the gift we give ourselves through sacrificial giving to others. . . . Single women can make lasting contributions in the lives of others by being involved in ministries of giving and serving."⁴ They tell of a single aunt who for years has organized family reunions. As this single woman ages, she knows she is entering a new season. She wants the reunions to continue, so she is teaching and encouraging the younger nieces and nephews to take over her job.

I am reminded of Barbara Bush's comments to the 1990 graduating class of Wellesley College. She was very aware of woman's ability to connect relationally.

> The . . . choice that must not be missed is to cherish your human connections: your relationships with friends and family. For several years, you've had impressed upon you the importance to your career of dedication and hard work. This is true, but as important as your obligations as a doctor, lawyer, or business leader will be, you are a human being first and those human connections—with spouses, with children, with friends—are the most important investments you will ever make. At the end of your life, you will never regret not having passed one more test, not winning one more verdict or not closing one more deal. You will regret time not spent with a husband, a friend, a child, or a parent.⁵

# Conclusion

Your connections keep the wheels of life on the road. Your hub work may not feel significant or fulfilling at times, but in reality, you are creating an environment of safety and confidence that enables a healthy future for both family and society. Through it all, your hub connections stabilize the drifting factors floating in your realm and allow security to be enjoyed.

Too important or too busy or too high powered to be a hub? Not anymore. We appreciate the opportunity to see benefits from our great influence!

# CHAPTER 13

# Connecting Past to Present and Future

When family members care for each other, for the young and for the seniors, we link the past to the present and the present to the future. One of our daughters-in-law has said repeatedly that she wants to take care of us in our old age, as we've cared for others for many years. As a practical expression of willingness to connect our generation to hers and to the future, she painted a picture for me with watercolors.

In the picture, my daughter depicts me leading her down a path to the ocean. It appears that we have previously climbed a hill together. The details bring the future alive before my eyes. Using symbolic colors, she has me dressed in deep purple and herself in lighter purple as we view a beautiful sunset over the water.

Over the scene of this painting she printed these words from the Book of Ruth: "Intreat me not to leave thee, or to return from following after thee: for whither thou goest, I will go; and where thou lodgest, I will lodge: thy people shall be my people, and thy God my God: Where thou diest, will I die, and there will I be buried: the LORD do so to me, and more also, if ought but death part thee and me" (1:16–17, KJV). Above her signature, she wrote, "I love you, Mom." I received her gift only days ago as I write. Today as I share with you this connection power we women have, I opened up the frame and found a further message on the back of the painting. "For Mom Weber, mother of my 'kinsman redeemer,' and my guide on God's path along womanhood. I love you beyond words, and am so thankful for you in my life. Your daughter, (and signed)."

With words and loving actions, a woman is able to make a significant connection from one generation to another. She is often gifted to use tangible treasures that make and preserve memories. Those physical items pass on the messages of love and care that are etched on the hearts of those who touched them earlier. Because many families are becoming so fragmented, it is important that we preserve the heirlooms that remind us of the good God has done and is doing in us.

# The Value of Connection

When we remember things, we make a connection between *what* and *why*. God initiated this idea for His people. When the Israelites passed through the Jordan River via God's miraculous parting of the waters, He told them to display stones that would remind them of their deliverance. When the Israelites were told to build the tabernacle, the physical structure was to be a reminder that it represented all that God is. Then in the New Testament we are asked to regularly make the connection between what God has done for us on the cross and why He did it by taking communion. We are to remember.

Enjoying strength in the present and future happens best when we hold on to what is good from the past. Especially when our world and circumstances are changing, we need to keep the strength of the past close by for reinforcement. We must not let the opportunity of passing good traits from one generation to another slip away. There are positive traits and skills that each of us can find from generations before us to pass down. Whether it is how to wallpaper, cook a turkey, make bead rings, or develop the fine art of communication, the ongoing generations need to learn. More essential than the simple skills are the character building and lessons of spiritual growth.

Taking time to be a grandmother to our grandchildren allows everybody to win. Our connections with them develop a bond that carries traditions of great family heritage. In the process, the self-esteem of the next generation soars. Recipes, the cross-stitched scenes, or all those birthday and holiday celebrations reflect something of importance. We all remember certain things about older persons—learning Bible verses, the tin of buttons, the gumdrop trees, the special dresses made for us, or lessons in how to braid hair. The tangible things remind us of the time we spent together, the messages of love toward us.

The feminine touch facilitates the opportunities for linking the past to the present and the future. At our house, one important event is the filling of stockings at Christmas. It takes all year to find those little treasures that will mean something to each recipient. Little things remind us of bigger things, and the message plays on in all of our minds to connect generations.

Our sons are all married now, so I thought it was time to stop hanging the advent calendar at Christmas. Since there were no more little (or big) boys to uncover the little Christmas symbol each day, I thought its purpose had been served. When one of my sons came through the house before Christmas, he said, "Where's the advent calendar?" It did make a difference to him. He loved that calendar. Its presence reminded him of former joys, and he missed it. Traditions are for generations to speak of legacy connection. You are a key player in the memory-making process.

# Connection Builds Adult Confidence

Barry Arnold, one of our fellow pastors, used to live as a missionary among the Alaskan people. The women of the Koyukon world in the interior of Alaska have an ancient custom they fulfill called "Pride Your Man."

They play a key role as young boys become men. It is interesting that they know that no man will rise above the expectations of the women around him.

> Wearing their best clothing they dance in a circle with their eyes focused on a young man in the center. The tradition is to give him confidence, through their increased energy exerted, increased pitch and intensity of song. They communicate approval in obvious ways to infuse his veins with strength and vigor. As the young man begins to feel accepted, believed in, promoted, admired, and encouraged, he becomes a confident leader that God intends for him to be. Everybody wins as these women fulfill the tradition to connect the young men to a strong future of leadership with confidence.[1]

# Treasuring People and Their Expressions

Women provide enrichment to life as they preserve history. They do this by treasuring people and their expressions. I wanted my boys to feel treasured, so I kept the things that were important to them. When they made pottery items in school, I saved them, and I use them even now. The books that were important to them were important to me. The traditions that were important to them were important to me—like making Rocky Road Fudge Squares for every holiday season.

I display Ryan's tattered teddy bear by a copy of *The Velveteen Rabbit*. The old favorite rocking horse is in the attic because the owner wants it for his children someday. I saved each lettered jacket in an honored place after they left home. I keep a file of all the boys' awards, letters of love, and special artwork.

Many of us have made special outfits for our children for school and church programs. Although we didn't think we had the time to do it, we did. "Although few of the masterpieces you have made survive childhood and achieve heirloom status, a mother who takes time to make *anything* for her child creates for him a lasting memory of her loving hands and attentive heart," says Sandy Lynam Clough.[2]

Because I treasure the family I married into, I've learned to treasure the special foods that they desire at holiday time. I learned that I needed to buy only Italian dry salami and not some other kind. Many years ago I offered to bring a pumpkin cake to the holiday celebration. Their family tradition was pumpkin pie. Now I prefer the pie too. I like to treasure the people I love by remembering their preferences. Foods, cooked and served like the generations before us, have a way of linking the past to the present. Proverbs 24: 4 tells us, "By knowledge the rooms are filled with all precious and pleasant riches."

## Collecting Treasures Increases Worth

A woman who accumulates memory makers increases her family's worth because "keeping is a gift of celebrating family. . . . She keeps the things that give her family a sense of continuity."[3] She is not a pack rat, but an extender of legacy.

In the book *The Memory Box*, Mary Kay Shanley describes the emotions as various generations wade through boxes of treasures. The biggest thought is that "memories are in the heart of the keeper, and as such, truly become treasures to pass on to generations that follow."[4]

Our home may be of traditional styling but the contents are a mixture of the old and the new. They reflect our lives and tell many stories. The treasures throughout tell where we've been, what we are about, and allow even a stranger to get to know us. One little plaque of anonymous origin says this:

> Our home is filled with objects dear
> And memories of yesteryear;
> But treasured even more than these,
> Is the love of our friends and families.

Next to that little saying, I have things displayed in little wooden holders used to hold cans when picking berries. For many years these holders were used in the area we have lived. In these I put the baby spoons and forks from each of our sons, along with my baby mush bowl. I also have my grandmother's darning egg, the light Grandpa wore in the coal mine, a record with my husband's voice when he was two years old, a very old family wedding certificate, old family eye glasses, an old report card, Grandma's camera that got us interested in photographing our memories, and other very old items of concern to our family.

Our loft has many items of memorabilia. We have family baby pictures, Grandma's teakettle, Great-grandpa's metal Pepsi carrier, and a very old Worcestershire bottle we dug up by an old gold mine on a vacation wilderness trip.

## Appreciation Magnified through Memories Collected

There is "a time to keep, and a time to throw away," Ecclesiastes 3:6 tells us. I love to reflect on stories of importance to my family. Since 1966 we've kept a guest book. It contains many friends' signatures, which remind us of special people and times. My silver charm bracelet and spoon racks each have almost one hundred reminders of stories behind them. My sixty-two photo albums reflect another connection from the past to the present. The baby and year-by-year schoolbooks, the collection of birthday and Christmas videos, and those of special sporting contests all tug our hearts.

I have saved various tapes of Stu's preaching for each son's family so they will have tangible memories in years to come. Things like old prayer lists I used over the years to pray for our friends and families are filed as reminders of the past. We had the "height chart" cut from the Sheetrock at our last house, so we could keep it to jog fun memories.

Since (selective) collecting is connecting, I want to take you into our front sitting room. I love my "Word of God" wall. On the mantle, among other things, are my grandma's Bible and Stu's grandpa's Bible. Much heritage rests there. Across the room is the piano that was in my grandparents' home. Above the piano is a framed piece of sheet music of "The Holy City" with Stu's grandmother's signature. Below the music in the same frame, I placed a photo of Grandma and Grandpa's fiftieth wedding anniversary and the house their children were born and grew up in. Our appreciation of people blossoms as we choose to appreciate the "pieces" of material that are associated with them.

Then there are the bookshelves, which are filled with favorite books. And filling in the bookshelves are more family treasures of every kind. Look around your home. You, too, can tell many stories by looking at the pictures and mementos you have.

# Why Should We Collect to Connect?

One of my daughters-in-law took flowers from her wedding, dried and glued them on a parchment with a personalized poem, and presented me this gift of her love. Besides the flowers connecting us to a blessed event of importance, the words expressed a union of our souls now tied together with ribbons of gratefulness. Her descriptions of my careful nurturing, which have prepared her husband to love her well, help me feel like I've helped connect the past to the present and the future.

Another daughter-in-law saved all the roses my son had given her during their courtship. She dried them and crafted them into pew decorations and centerpieces for the tables at the wedding reception. Why? They were beautiful, and she was thrifty. But most important, when the guests saw the flowers and heard the story behind them, they realized more keenly how much love there was between this bride and groom. Collecting and displaying mementos creates feelings and jogs memories. They remind us of the love behind them, and they bring that love to life again. When we have missing links in our understanding, they connect the dots for us. Such pieces represent an era, a season, an honor, an event, an experience, or a memory that has relationship behind it all. And they keep the memory alive.

You pass down an attitude about life when you consider memory making to be a good investment of your time, talents, and money. Before I knew who my boys would marry, I purchased a church cookbook for each girl. I wanted them to enjoy a connection with so many great women whose favorite recipes were presented.

A Ph.D. candidate did research on the value of photographs and what they accomplish. Photographs

> are proof-positive that a child has a place in life and relationships with others. [They] indicate caring, nurturing, love and success . . . provide a sense of personal history . . . enhance feeling of safety or offer stimulation . . . supply someone young with tangible security . . . evoke a strong sense of self . . . [help] the viewer to feel more connected . . . help recapture memories of happiness . . . and reinforce a child's feeling of being both loved and capable.[5]

# What Do Women Do to Connect?

Women have more ways of connecting than a man could imagine—it's who we are. We'll leave notes on a pillow, turn a bed down for a loved one, or take breakfast in bed to one who needs the encouragement. Maybe we'll help a friend find a piece of furniture or whatever. We send cards to express everything (ask the card makers about the staggering statistics). Women enjoy secret sisters and pen pals. We feel, we express, we show care because we need to connect. Aloneness is not part of a woman's profile.

I've been to numerous women's retreats and seen the kind of work women have done all year long to get ready for these events. They make intricate name tags and elaborate door signs. There are personalized gifts on each bed and special works of art for the speaker. When I tell my husband, he says, "Don't they have anything better to do with their time?" But to women, such efforts are a valued use of time.

One of my daughters-in-law is learning and loving the art of quilting. Each type of quilt speaks a different message, for there is much history behind each of the patterns. Quilts connect us to generations gone before. It meant the world to me when my grandmother gave me a quilt she had made, and the boys' grandma gave each of them quilts as well. Each time I see a quilt, I am moved by the work that has gone into it. Because of the powerful statement a quilt makes, the women of our church present every first-time mother with a handmade quilt.

I think of my grandmother every time I use a set of name cards at the table. I glued a piece of her beautiful batting across the top of each card. I love seeing a touch of her every time we use those.

Another medium that women use to connect is to give their daughters a hope chest to hold memorable gifts for future use. I didn't have a chest, but Mom worked hard to get silverware for my future use. We saved coupons and collected them from friends for many years, so we could eventually get the whole set. Mom wanted to prepare me to leave home and to have something from home to connect with the future.

## Making Statements from the Heart

We had some friends staying with us one summer when they received a call informing them that Mom (and Grandmother to some) had died. It was hard for them to be so far away from home and deal with this loss. Words are inadequate in these moments. Music affords a connection in soothing the soul or renewing hope. I decided to step to the piano and play some of the old hymns of the faith, "Great Is Thy Faithfulness," "Faith Is the Victory," and "Amazing Grace." It seemed to be the right mode of connection as we remembered this dear faithful saint.

I love watching these daughters of mine use their feminine bent to make statements from their hearts in their homes. Not only do they all use music well, but the statement of appreciation for past heritage is expressed in multiple fashions. One of the girls tastefully displays touches from her farm background. She has used hoes and rakes and shovels as rods for artistic curtains. She decorated with flour sacks and a literal pallet on the wall. A lot is communicated when people come into rooms that truly make statements from the heart.

# Take the Good, Connect It, and Leave the Rest

Someday Jesus is going to take from our works what is good, connect them to a reward, and leave the rest. He's going to apply a type of spiritual blowtorch to our life and all the chaff will be burned. What remains will be wonderful. Regardless of our background, we can take all the good seeds we find, fertilize them, provide a good environment, and make some good new connections. We can multiply the joy in our life.

About the bad seeds, we can acknowledge their presence. Don't dwell on them, or allow them to get developed. Most everybody has hard stories. Plow them under and start making fine soil that will provide links to a positive future.

Proverbs 8:20–21 says, "'I walk in the way of righteousness, / In the midst of the paths of justice, . . . That I may fill their treasuries.'"

"As time passes, do our memories get left behind in empty rooms and gardens left untended? Or can we carry them with us and transplant them in the rich soil of a new life to bear new blossoms?"[6] The choices are ours.

Keep the good memories alive by passing the baton of a strong heritage. We reflect God's light as we make heritage connections.

❧

# PART 5

# Facet #4

# Designer Meant to Beautify

## CHAPTER 14

# The Wonderful Female Body

W o-man!" Men have been exclaiming this with exuberance since the beginning of time. And all cultures have a universal theme—that beauty be preeminent. We possess an insatiable desire to make the body look good, feel good, and smell good. (Oh, that we had the same drive to *be* good as well.)

I grew up in a conservative church where physical beauty was definitely not a focus. The verse in Proverbs 31:30, "Charm is deceitful and beauty is vain, / *But* a woman who fears the LORD, she shall be praised," was highly esteemed. I agree that the internal development of fearing the Lord should be encouraged before any outward focus. Inner self-esteem through strength in God is a form of beauty that takes priority over externals. We probably all know a woman who is not pretty but who radiates an internal loveliness of character. It is a pleasure to be around such a person.

192

# Reflecting God's Image

We need to have a balance in everything. Our bodies are important. God created our bodies in His image (*Our* image, says the Bible, plural persons of God in one—the mystery of the Trinity). Genesis 1:26–27 says, "Then God said, 'Let Us make man in Our image, according to Our likeness; and let them rule over the fish of the sea and over the birds of the sky and over the cattle and over all the earth, and over every creeping thing that creeps on the earth.' And God created man in His own image, in the image of God He created him; male and female He created them."

Isn't it interesting that "the LORD God formed man of dust from the ground" (Gen. 2:7). Then in appreciating the flair He intended to express through the female creation, the Scriptures say, "And the LORD God fashioned into a woman the rib which He had taken from the man" (Gen. 2:22). God designed her. He fashioned her. He planned that she would be different from the man. She could reflect God's image through her beautiful body. God initiated this fashioning process, and women have expanded the territory ever since.

Remember how God pronounced each aspect of His creation "good." The only thing that was pronounced "not good" was "for the man to be alone" (Gen. 2:18). Can't you see God smiling as He unveiled the presentation of this masterpiece? God planned for both man and woman to reflect the image of God, in unique ways.

# Physical Expression of the Spiritual

Is it legitimate to discuss the body in relation to feminine beauty? Certainly. You can't talk about femininity and not talk about the beautiful female body. In *The Woman Behind the Mirror*, Judith Couchman writes, "I've needed to celebrate the God-endowed face and body that is uniquely and utterly mine."[1] We need to remember that there is a physical side to being spiritual.

For the believer in Christ, we are told in 1 Corinthians 6:15, "Your bodies are members of Christ." Furthermore, "Your body is a temple of the

Holy Spirit who is in you, whom you have from God, and that you are not your own[.] For you have been bought with a price" (1 Cor. 6:19–20). So you see, we have a large obligation to take care of our bodies. We need to make the most of what we've been given to do justice to being a proper vessel that houses the living God.

# The Physical Body

The female body is the perfect place to start when dealing with the fourth facet of femininity—the Designer.

God designed woman's attractive curves and soft skin. There is power in the beauty of a woman, and advertisers know that. Female beauty speaks. It sends messages. It attracts response. It invokes appreciation.

If you have spent time reading Song of Songs, you have been exposed to some rather graphic descriptions of this body. I'll never forget a wedding we attended where the couple chose to have twenty minutes of reading from this book. People squirmed in their seats and looked at their watches. Every part of the body was described as a pleasant picture or experience. The bride and groom expressed their passionate desires to experience each other's body. It would do every married couple good to rehearse these Scriptures together. It could keep them anticipating the physical oneness that is intended for pleasure in the marriage relationship.

No body talk is ever complete without mentioning sexual realities, although that is not our focus here. I have previously encouraged married women to do everything they can to enhance their sex lives with their husbands. We must never forget that we were designed for sex—the procreation that occurs during our union with the man and the pleasure God intends each partner to experience in the marriage relationship.

God designed men to be indescribably attracted to women's bodies in a strong way. I marvel how God gave us this magnetic pull to sustain intrigue over time. Sometimes we women wonder why God made our focus so different from the man's. The sexual experience that God designed includes many physical and emotional differences. A man is visually stimulated and body oriented, and his desire for sex is among his top needs. We don't need to take a survey to tell us that. A woman is stimulated by touch and needs to feel secure and safe before enjoying sex. Another part of our sexual nature is the cycle we go through monthly and the PMS that sometimes affects us. It is an area about which we should become knowledgeable.

# Taking Care of Your Body

When I was a little girl, I watched the Miss America pageant. Those women were so beautiful. Although I didn't possess the raw material to pursue such titles, I mentally cast myself into the fairy-tale role of being one of those poised and talented finalists. I wanted to develop that feminine aura, which I saw so beautifully presented.

The body is an incredible design of God. Daily we have the privilege to make the most of what we've been given. By being designed beautifully as women, we, in turn, become designers to beautify ourselves and the world around us.

Maintenance is a biblical principle that applies in every area of life. We would never buy a house or car and not take care of it. We spend money on preventing problems, on insurance in case things come up, and on repairs as needs arise.

God gives us a body and expects us to maintain it. We take precautions by eating the right foods and avoiding unhealthy ones. We exercise and even "pump iron." (Prov. 31:17 says, "She girds herself with strength, / And makes her arms strong.") We discipline ourselves to get adequate sleep. These are the basics.

One day when I was thirty-six, I was standing in line to use a bathroom in a hotel. I had been visiting with a friend as we waited in line. When I stopped speaking, a total stranger behind me said, "Excuse me, but I've been watching you." She paid me some nice compliments and then asked, "Have you ever considered having orthodontic work done?" Not many folks are bold enough to ask such a question. I was taken aback. It was almost like telling someone she needs plastic surgery on her ugly face. I thought she must be a new orthodontist looking for somebody on which she could practice.

I told her, "I have one son in braces now and more coming up, so I haven't considered asking that I take the priority for the family's money to be spent on me."

"I work in dentistry and so I notice people's teeth," she said. "I just thought you would really enjoy what braces would do for you."

I didn't think too much about it at the time. Later as I told my husband about the conversation, he asked if I would like to get braces. One thing led to another, and somehow my husband made that possible for me. And I've been grateful ever since for that opportunity to look my best—even after four years of head gear and appliances.

# Enhancing the Body

I never had the opportunity to attend charm school as I grew up, but I think it would be a wonderful thing for little girls to learn how to carry themselves gracefully. It would enhance the body for life. When a young lady learns how to stand and sit and walk with dignity, she reflects beauty. It is like putting an expensive frame on a nice picture to start with, making the finished product magnificent. And because most things in life that are valuable require work, most women will expend some effort in learning to enhance their natural beauty.

Remember, I grew up in a very conservative church. We were not taught physical ways to enhance beauty. Outward appearance was downplayed, and only abstract spiritual qualities were considered worthy of developing. You can observe a biblical charm course as you consult the book of Esther. Those beautiful ladies, who were brought to King Ahasuerus, spent twelve months getting ready for such an event. Esther 2:12 says, "For the days of their beautification were completed as follows: six months with oil of myrrh and six months with spices and the cosmetics for women." Esther 2:15 says, "And Esther found favor in the eyes of all who saw her." In *Why Beauty Matters*, Karen Lee-Thorp and Cynthia Hicks compare Jezebel's pride to Esther's humility in their beautification processes.

> Compare Jezebel's arrogance to Esther's three days of humble fasting before she adorned herself to face King

Ahasuerus. Esther wasn't interested in exalting herself above other women or triumphing over anyone but the evil Haman, but Jezebel craved her own aggrandizement at everyone else's expense. Esther knew she merely reflected God's glory; Jezebel lusted for her own glory. Pride is the normal human desire for respect swollen to an obsession with status, the normal human longing for love bloated into a demand for worship.[2]

Does that sound like it is appropriate for us to spend some time, energy, and even purchase some cosmetics to enhance the beauty God has blessed us with naturally? Yes, it is spoken to. Let's make sure we choose to be women of balance first, reflecting the beauty of a pleasant, becoming woman of God who demonstrates discretion. We may have a lot more to learn than we even realized.

# Learning to Make the Most of What We're Given

I have pictures of Mom french-braiding my hair, an art I'll hopefully get to practice on granddaughters. When I went away to school, I lived down the hall from a girl who had been offered the lead hairdresser job at 20th Century Fox Studios in Hollywood. I watched her carefully for a year. That ability I acquired from her later enabled me to pursue a business venture while my husband was in Vietnam for a year. But more importantly, it has helped me to care for my appearance as well.

There is a biblical principle we can follow with this: Make the most of what we've been given. Acquiring even small tips will help you do justice to the body you have been given—tips regarding:

- Face shapes and the better way to cut and style your hair.
- Seasonal coloring of your skin tone, for making better choices of colors to use or wear.
- Body sizes and shapes, to minimize and maximize needed areas with clothing choices.

# Looking Your Best

Dressing well doesn't require a lot of money for clothes. It is an art. You can learn to develop this art by studying what other people do well, and how.

Let me tell you about my Aunt Ada. She is eighty-five years old and totally blind after seeing very little most of her life. Her husband died in tragic circumstances years ago, and she has always lived with meager means, now having only her Social Security stipend. With her five-foot-ten-inch frame and weighing in at less than one hundred pounds, she lives with a challenge to look good. And yet she has always made the most of everything, including her appearance. She is not vain. She rarely has a visitor. I love getting to travel to her city, surprise her in that tiny little room, and see this joyful human being. She looks like a million dollars and yet achieves this on a peasant's pay. She has few shopping privileges and little storage to even own many clothes. What she wears is clean, matches, and is always well chosen. Her hair looks like she just walked out of the beauty shop. You would think she is expecting someone to take her out on the town. There are a lot of lessons to be learned from Ada's attitude and abilities. Above all, her appearance illustrates her feeling about life. She's grateful for another day and she likes to look the part of that gratefulness, that feminine celebration.

# More Than Permission from Scripture

Again, Scripture gives us insight. The Proverbs 31 lady had clothing of fine linen and purple. First Peter 3:3 takes for granted the expression of external beauty, mentioning the woman's braided hair and her wearing of gold jewelry and fine dresses. But this only prefaces the true beauty that develops in the hidden person of the heart. Both inner and outer beauty is spoken of favorably. Where inner development is obviously essential, there is an assumption that the externals were cared for. Do not forget to praise God for the body with which He has blessed you. Enhancing and appreciating this outward beauty in a healthy way glorifies Him through beauty that dwells within.

# Principles Made Practical

It is smart for you to beautify your body through the means of clothing. It's best not to let yourself wear dirty, torn, or run-down items. Things that fit right will always be your best choice. Instead of allowing that frequent phrase to come from your lips, "I don't have a thing to wear," maybe you might do as my little niece, Katie, did and check out the local second-hand store. She found a new swimsuit for a dollar or so. And when the family was enjoying some time in the hot tub together, four-year-old Katie sat on the edge, gazing at "her new look" and said, "Don't I look just great?" We can learn much from the freshness of a child.

There is a lot one can learn to continue the beautification process:

- Hair coloring, cuts, curls, and removal of unwanted hair
- Nails
- Makeup and skin care
- Fragrance, oils
- Jewelry and other accessories

Learning to apply makeup is an art. You can diminish your weaknesses and enhance your strengths. It can be subtle or almost amusing. I have done a little TV work. In preparation for appearing "on the set," you are required to go through a makeup session. All of your features are heavily enhanced so you will come across with specific definition. Although it is fun to see what they can do with you, I always felt a bit overdone.

One evening one of my friends wanted to take me to a dress-up community service event. In the process, she thought it would be fun if we "got a makeover." I have always enjoyed wearing makeup and learning how to do it well, but this time I couldn't quit laughing inside. After the makeover, I was having my nails done. I couldn't help but think that the technician was ready to burst into laughter. I told her, "Miss, this is not really me. I just got a makeover." My appearance embarrassed me to the point of apologizing to a total stranger.

There are extremes to everything—too much, too little, maybe nothing. Learning how to do it well is always a good idea. When you learn to be subtle and yet skillfully definitive, you create a pleasurable effect. Suddenly you become like a picture that was rather nondescript. When the picture gets placed in an elegant frame there is new appreciation for the art. Previously, people hadn't realized the beauty of the picture.

# Framing Your Artwork

God wants us to become knowledgeable about proper framing for our artwork. He created our bodies, and He desires that we learn to make the most of our appearance. Choose a kind of background for yourself that sets you up for maximum effectiveness. Your husband will get excited. Your children will be proud. Your coworkers will appreciate the care you give to provide a total package of proper pride.

Looking good to please God is biblical. Contentedness in pleasing Him will nullify any body hatred, such as the fear of looking old, or trends of anorexia, bulimia, or other unhealthy obsessions/concerns. Living out a God-focus ensures your body is in order. Creating beauty as a designer for God is a worthwhile mission. There is theology to it all, for "whatever you do, do all to the glory of God" (1 Cor. 10:31).

## CHAPTER 15

# Transforming Fragments into Beauty

$\mathcal{T}$he designer facet reflects light from the Source to a watching world who loves what they see. Physically, woman was created beautiful to behold. In turn, she has the ability to enhance whatever she touches. A quick look around points to the universal feminine tendency to nest, create, and beautify her environment. "No gray, drab world for God. He said, in effect, 'Let's dress it up.' And women have been doing the same ever since—making things beautiful. 'Hanging curtains on the bare windows of earth,'" says my husband, Stu, in *Tender Warrior*.[1]

From clothes to decor to flowers to table settings, woman communicates feeling and mood. She exudes a flair for frill as an unmistakable feminine expression, and God is smiling as she complements the man. One woman approached me as I spoke at a FamilyLife Conference and said, "I didn't expect you to be so feminine. You wear jewelry and are such a lady and yet you only have boys at your house." It's not our environment that reflects our femininity, it's who we are. Granted, my guys didn't always understand my bent to express myself so differently. As I have developed a growing understanding of this facet of femininity, I've gained new appreciation for it and freedom to enjoy what comes so naturally.

## The Lord's Example for Us

God is so good to give us such unique pictures of Himself for us to emulate. God is a designer who beautifies. He created man out of nothing. He created order out of void. He brought beauty out of chaos. He provides shelter in the time of storm—a refuge. "Throughout Scripture, God is referred to as our spiritual refuge. We are told to run to him for safety, security, rest, replenishment, comfort, and never-ending love. In the same way, I believe God created our homes to be our physical refuge," says Terry Willits.[2]

John 14:1–4 tells us not to let our hearts be troubled, but to believe in Him: "'In My Father's house are many dwelling places; if it were not so, I would have told you; for I go to prepare a place for you. And if I go and prepare a place for you, I will come again, and receive you to Myself; that where I am, there you may be also.'" He's making a nest for us so we'll be comfortable, be at home, have our needs met, and have a safe place to rest.

## Following the Creator's Lead

Our Designer is the plumb line we need to copy. We also get the privilege of preparing a place—our homes. Susan Hunt offers these thoughts:

> The virtue of domesticity begins with an untroubled heart that has been redeemed from sin and is focused on our heavenly home. This virtue is expressed as we prepare places on earth that depict our heavenly home. This is accomplished as we reflect the character of Jesus in our homes and churches, thus making them homey places

where troubled hearts find rest and safety. So domestic deeds are rooted in our theology.[3]

A prepared place feels like you and yours, not like somebody else or their stuff. Tracy Porter helps us enjoy the thought of making our homes a precious place to be.

> I've long thought it peculiar that people will freely substitute the words "home" and "house." To me, one is an empty canvas; the other a soul-revealing portrait. One a ream of blank paper; the other a masterpiece of literature. Home is an unceasing experiment into the temperament of beauty—capturing it, focusing it—and releasing it for reinterpretation. Home is sanctuary, inspiration, and a living tribute to all of life's shared and personal glories, as well as its quiet moments of reappraisal, even sorrow. Home is a reflection of my loves, my spirit, and my soul. It is not merely where I live; it is where my life is.[4]

How fun it is to create feelings of warmth. As a designer, it takes work. Why do you suppose realtors like to sell houses when they remain decorated with the expressions of people living there? Our hearts are warmed by homes that present a cozy feeling. Maybe it's a fragrance or a picture that brings back memories. Maybe the smell of cider brewing or the glow of the Christmas tree lets us almost hear the laughter of the family.

# Creating a Nest

Most of us have watched female birds "fussing" to make their nests for the cute little birds yet to arrive. They hustle back and forth with such diligence. Their clever design work amazes us; their ability to know how to weave twigs, grass, and other discarded fragments into a tight, soft nest appears to be inborn. How can they be so good at what they do?

Most girls start learning to beautify things when they are young. My sister, Judy, and I played house. We didn't have a fancy place to play. We made our own little nest out of large boxes. We fixed them up just right to be "our house." I had a little kid "stove" that actually fried an egg (ever so slowly), so we thought we had a wonderful nest.

You know what it's like moving into a new place. You want to arrange things so you can use them easily and so they look good. You take time and effort to get it just right, for you. When I am traveling and going to be in a hotel room for several days, I have a smaller-scale nesting party. Terry Willits, who is an interior designer and pastor's wife, says this, "One thing I have learned about women: God has designed all of us with a desire to create a nest. . . . It is a great privilege to help clients transform their homes into places that bring them pleasure and peace of mind."[5]

# Making Something Out of What We Have

Your nest doesn't need to be a decorator's showroom. You don't need a large budget to make nice things happen. The secret of nesting well is to take what you have and make something of it. It's a little like the mustard seed. "'If you have faith as a mustard seed, you shall say to this mountain, "Move from here to there," and it shall move; and nothing shall be impossible to you'" (Matt. 17:20). Let your mustard seed go to work for you— you might be surprised with the extravaganza that takes place.

I grew up in a tiny migrant farm shelter. No carpet. The cement floor shower had uncleanable walls of linoleum. No forced air furnace. What we had was less than what people living on welfare possess today. We stored our things in apple boxes, covered with grandmother's embroidered cloths. We learned to be clever in adding flair to our life. Where there is a will, there is a way to express our feminine bent. If beauty is expressed with only meager means and a healthy attitude, that beauty can be comely.

We lived at least the first twenty years of our marriage quite meagerly. I longed for opportunities to be a more sophisticated designer. I thought, *If we ever have any extra money, I'll decorate more and have a few more clothes or fancy foods.* But I learned how to "make do" and to watch miracles take place over our "five loaves" to feed the hardy appetites in our home. I made charts to track our finances. Spending only fifty dollars for a whole month for five of us proves that miracles did take place regularly. My theme song for the boys was, "Be thankful for the good things that you've got."

Over the years, we have had many people in our home. In order to feed them something special when I had no money to buy nice food, I needed to be creative. We could pick wild (free) blackberries in season and freeze them for pies. People would occasionally give us a salmon, which I always put away for guests. When my gardening friends offered their produce, I blanched and froze everything. We actually did very well on very little for a long time. I can tell similar stories about clothes, furniture, and decor. My wish to beautify did not go unmet because I had little money.

Let's look at the Proverbs 31 woman:

| *Took what she had* | *and* | *made something of it.* |
|---|---|---|
| v. 16 took her earnings | | and planted a vineyard |
| v. 17 took her body | | girded herself with strength |
| v. 18 took her lamp | | didn't let it go out at night |
| v. 19 used her hands | | to run a spindle |
| v. 20 used her hands | | to extend to the poor and needy |
| v. 21 used her hands | | and made familiar clothes of scarlet |
| v. 22 used her hands | | and made herself clothes of fine linen |
| v. 24 used her hands | | to make garments and sell them and to supply belts to tradesmen |
| v. 25 used her life | | to choose strength and dignity |

So then, we can create a lot of beauty by using the straw we have available. Out of nothing, or very little, we can make much. Our good attitude is the most necessary ingredient.

# Create a Tapestry

There's an old Greek proverb that says, "To possess ideas is to gather flowers; To think is to weave them into garlands." Life hands us a lot of loose pieces. Our job is to take those pieces and weave them into something beautiful.

"My home is more than a place to live; it is the one place where I can truly create. . . . I am the artist who makes my house home," says Tracy Porter.[6] She also says this about the work we accomplish at home: "Home is a living memory book of tears and smiles, laughter, whispers, song. Home is where honesty and realness hold forth. At home, we know and we are known."[7]

You may become more of an artist than you ever thought possible. Your soul wants to express the pieces in and around you. Go ahead. Make a tapestry. Let your heart tie the themes together and express the interests of those around you. Display what is important to you. Make a statement about your values. All the fragments are beautiful pieces to be woven together. That kind of work expresses your heart and reflects light from the God who designed you.

# Putting Zest into the Ordinary

Without zest, the fragments remain just that. Sandy Lynam Clough tells of a special joy in her life—"the joy of inspiration, the joy of heart and hand working together in a sometimes-sacrificial labor of love, the joy of creating, the joy that comes with sharing those efforts, and the joy that people receive from our gift. I have found this joy in work done with needle and thread, but that is only one of many paths of creativity."[8]

The designer conveys feelings of importance in her tasks in life, whether they be handwork projects, food presentations, decor work, or clothing statements. Adding tidbits of beauty enhances any experience. During a trip to New England with Mom and Dad Weber, we observed the power of small touches of artistry. Mom had anticipated eating lobster in Maine. The day finally came when her dream came true in a quaint little restaurant on the oceanfront at Kennebunkport.

Her lobster was cooked just right. It was arranged on the plate quite precisely with other delicacies. Even the salad was crisp and lightly tossed with just the right herbs and the right amount of mayonnaise. She will never forget that meal.

Later that same trip, she ordered lobster at another restaurant. The sign outside looked inviting, but that was the end of the pleasure. They used paper plates, the lobster was rubbery, the seasoning lacked flavor, and the food was just "plopped" in front of us. No frills, no thrills. We left feeling uncared for.

You can put zest into ordinary meals at home, into ordinary outfits, and into arrangement of the furniture. As we allow our artistic bent to influence our world, we communicate caring. The feelings we create transform mere fragments into beauty.

# Learning by Watching Others

I didn't learn about design as I grew up. Yet we are born with an inclination to "hang curtains on the bare windows of earth." Since there's "nothing new under the sun,"[9] we can learn a lot by watching how people around us create beauty. Take that natural bent of yours to "fuss over things" and develop it. When we were getting ready to build our home, I subscribed to a number of magazines so I could learn from others.

I've been watching my mother-in-law (Dorothy Weber) decorate for years, and she's good. She is always coming up with new ways to make beautiful changes, and on a tight budget. My sister and then my daughters-in-law have taught me a lot too, and they were trained to do it well by watching their moms. My friend, Betty Holmlund, has been influencing me for twenty-seven years with her incredible talent to combine colors and textures.

Transforming fragments into beauty is an art to be developed from our inborn creative juices. As we observe other people do it well, we can enhance our abilities to reflect even greater light through this facet of femininity.

# Beauty that Shines Deeply and Brightly

The kind of beauty we have been talking about will help a woman build her house. Proverbs 14:1 offers us that wisdom: "The wise woman builds her house." Essentially, the foolish woman leaves everything in fragments. It takes a lot of work to pull the pieces together. When we treasure something, we place our heart there. "'For where your treasure is, there will your heart be also'" (Matt. 6:21). So then, beauty emerges through having our treasure in the right places, with all the hidden meanings coming through to prepare a house as Jesus would.

### Patchwork of Beauty

The patchwork of a life that's lived
With grace and charm each day;
Reflects the light creatively
God planned just as He may.

A woman's touch adds life to
All those plain old walls so bare.
She takes those cold bare window frames
And uses her feminine flair

To paint a picture full of life
That expresses her heart so well;
Her family, friends, and guests alike
Find warmth to their every cell.

The beauty of unique design
Adds color to the soul;
As woman creates her masterpiece
With emotions to enfold

Our hearts detailed with ecstasy,
From filling in the blanks;
Where once we only basics knew,
To God we must give our thanks.

—Linda Weber

# CHAPTER 16

# *Expression Made through Details*

$\mathcal{E}$ach of our sons went to Wheaton College, which was two thousand miles away from home. As upperclassmen, each of them lived in a college house with many other guys. They loved every minute of this new opportunity and could hardly wait to show us where they lived. When we entered that first son's house, I'll not forget my response (which I kept to myself). I was happy that they were elated with their living situation, but it lacked a lot in my opinion. Being a woman, I would have chosen to decorate it differently.

They were enjoying great relationships—that was wonderful. But the old house was one year from being condemned. There was not one curtain in the place. And they liked it that way! They kept their things in boxes because they lacked furniture. There were no bedspreads or comforters. Bicycles filled the living room. No pictures graced the walls. Things were hanging from here and there, and I felt badly for my son. Details that would have been important to me made no difference to him or his housemates.

I remember when a male friend was about to get married. His bride-to-be decided his bachelor "pad" needed work. She transformed the place. Now it showed a woman's touch. It was so different that our friend couldn't get to sleep in his own bedroom for several nights.

Even though Stu and I have been married a long time, he still expresses how some decorative touch feels unnecessary. Yes, we do look at details differently. I sometimes joke with him, "Do you want to be married to a woman or a man?" We will always have different viewpoints, and so we have continual opportunity to flex with each other's differences. It is not only OK to be different, it is God's design.

## Differences with Details Keep Us Smiling

Whether we're working with details to create beauty or to express our feelings, the same principle applies. Consider these two versions of a new haircut.

*Women's version:*

WOMAN 2: Oh! You got a haircut! That's so cute!

WOMAN 1: Do you think so? I wasn't sure when she gave me the mirror. I mean, you don't think it's too fluffy looking?

WOMAN 2: Oh, no! It's perfect. I'd love to get my hair cut like that, but I think my face is too wide. I'm pretty much stuck with this stuff, I think.

WOMAN 1: Are you serious? I think your face is adorable. And you could easily get one of those layer cuts—that would look so cute, I think. I was actually going to do that except that I was afraid it would accent my long neck.

WOMAN 2: Oh—that's funny! I'd love to have your neck! Anything to take attention away from this two-by-four I have for a shoulder line.

WOMAN 1: Are you kidding? I know girls that would love to have your shoulders. Everything drapes so well on you. I mean, look at my arms—see how short they are? If I had your shoulders, I could get clothes to fit me so much easier.

~~~~~~~~~~~~~~~~~~~~~~

*Men's version:*

MAN 2: Haircut?

MAN 1: Yeah.[1]

Women love details, even if they are off the main subject. Men, on the other hand, like to get to the point. Sometimes men don't see the point of decorating, as it deals with "unnecessary details and expense." My mom wrote a letter to us about a wonderful luncheon she had attended. As I was reading this aloud to Stu (descriptions of everything at the table that day, including the details of how each item of food was served), I could tell that he was ready to get to the next "item of business" in the letter. Women love the details.

# God Is "Into" Details

God cares for the sparrows and about your hair count. "Are not two sparrows sold for a cent? And yet not one of them will fall to the ground apart from your Father. But the very hairs of your head are all numbered. . . . You are of more value than many sparrows" (Matt. 10:29–31).

God created women's brains with a capacity for details. God determined that women have more crossover connections between the left and right side of their brains, allowing an incredible detail orientation.

Neuroanatomist Laura Allen and neuroendocrinologist Roger Gorski of UCLA obtained live brain scans that have

> confirmed that parts of the corpus callosum were up to 23% wider in women than in men. They also measured thicker connections between the two hemispheres in other parts of women's brains. Encouraged by the discovery of such structural differences, many researchers have begun looking for dichotomies of function as well. At the Bowman Gray Medical School in Winston-Salem, N.C., Cecile Naylor has determined that men and women enlist

widely varying parts of their brain when asked to spell words. By monitoring increases in blood flow, the neuropsychologist found that women use both sides of their head when spelling while men use primarily their left side. Because the area activated on the right side is used in understanding emotions, the women apparently tap a wider range of experience for their task.[2]

We women sometimes become perturbed that men can't find something that we might easily locate. "In experiments in mock offices, women proved 70% better than men at remembering the location of items found on a desktop."[3] There is actually a brain difference that causes this.

A study also reveals that women remember more facts on charts. When men and women studied twenty-seven objects in a group for one minute, the women remembered an average of fifteen objects compared to twelve for the men.[4]

Men and women were also exposed to four simple words and then asked to name as many synonyms as possible in three minutes. The women could name an average of 4.1 synonyms per word compared to the men's average of 2.2 synonyms per word.[5]

These differences are not something to cause pride. The man indeed has strengths that are different from ours. One is their ability to think in three dimensions. "Whether men read maps better is unclear, but they do excel at thinking in three dimensions."[6] We must never become haughty or disappointed about differences—simply enjoy them for God's best purposes.

# Detailed Artistic Bent Seen Early

Little girls display their designer talents early. They want to wear cute little frilly shirts, smocked dresses, and patent-leather shoes with lacy socks. Poofy hair bows and matching barrettes add beauty to the braids or beautiful curls they've prepared. Finishing touches might be a coordinating purse and a delicate bracelet and/or necklace. (This is all quite different from what I experienced with my three sons. A pair of jeans and a T-shirt was all they wanted.)

Little girls grow up and continue to beautify themselves with more sophistication. They enjoy hair coloring, frosts, highlights, and length and style changes. Fingernails and toenails are painted. Jewelry becomes a fun option.

# Beautification Details Are Everywhere

For a season, during the boys' high school and college years, I worked at a large retail department store. Every day I enjoyed getting to help choose outfits for women in "my" Better Sportswear section. It was a lot of fun being a designer. Even better, I didn't have to spend money to enjoy all the flair.

While working there, I couldn't help but notice the square footage that is dedicated to a woman's beautification (clothing, shoes, accessories, foundations, sleepwear, cosmetics, and jewelry, not to mention the home beautification departments—linens, kitchen needs, furniture, etc.). The bulk of a store is indeed designed for women, because we do the shopping. Woman's orientation toward the details of beautification dictates how much of the money is spent in retail venues. Most of us could look at our closets and chuckle over how much space we use compared to the space men need.

I love setting a pretty table. Over the years I've accumulated large sets of dishes, so I can provide variety at our dining table. Decorating a table allows the use of many fun pieces: a centerpiece, candles, a runner, placemats, cloth napkins with napkin rings, name cards, matching favors, and all the right silverware. I love changing the options. And to be able to serve dinners well, I consult several of my cookbooks (and I have over one hundred) to combine just the right details.

Those of you who sew know how many pieces are required to make a finished product. You need a pattern, the right fabric, appropriate thread, the right buttons, appropriate length zipper, interfacing, bias tape, and several kinds of trim. Details provide beauty.

My latest beautification project has been to plan our new home. I had never had this option before, but I have enjoyed the new arena. Little things added here and there give the home that special touch. Had I not incorporated some details ahead of time, they would never have happened. For example, I wanted two sections in the dining room to have a plate rail, each with an electric outlet up high to facilitate a string of lights year-round.

I also chose a leaf theme that appears in the kitchen-tile backsplash, in several chandeliers, and in the outside lighting. Color themes tie one room into another and yet give each room its own "feel."

One detail that was important to me was what I call my "chapel" area. I wanted a quiet place where I would be undistracted when meeting with the Lord. That area simply lies in the corner of our bedroom where there is a comfortable chair and table for my Bible and other materials. I have a view of Mount Hood in one direction and a garden scene in the other.

# Details Speak Meaning

Building a house means paying attention to many physical details. Turning a house into our home requires paying "attention to its details so that it will not only remain intact, but stand firm," says Terry Willits in her book, *Creating a SenseSational Home.*[7] She goes on to name a few details that must not be avoided—noticing when someone needs to be held, cleaning out the refrigerator, and dropping a love note in a lunch bag. Maybe it means figuring out how to have a talk, so a hurting person can unload burdens. Maybe it means repeatedly looking into another's eyes with a smile on your face. Honoring these emotional details speaks deep meaning.

My friend Linda was always creative in expressing her love to her family. She left notes written with licorice sticks. She also wrote notes of love on the bathroom mirror with lipstick. Most of us have made those fun pancakes that have little messages or figures for our children. Details express love and increase feelings of worth—something you can do well. "And by knowledge the rooms are filled / With all precious and pleasant riches" (Prov. 24:4).

Think of the smile that comes when you make or serve foods that mean a lot to someone. I know I can win certain hearts with meatloaf, maple bars, sour apple candies, Lucky Charms, pizza, Cinnabons, biscotti, Sees candies, beef anything, strawberry crepes, mashed potatoes, or my gourmet cold raspberry soup.

Details calm a spirit. They add warmth. They feel fun and invite pleasure, so let's enjoy them.

## Men Often Don't Understand

Many men can't relate to our interest in details. Intellectually, we can learn of the other's way, but practically, it remains amusing. Stu will say, "I have no idea how you can remember that," or "Why don't we just skip so many of those things that take so much time."

Men sometimes give women a hard time about shopping. Not every woman likes to shop, I realize. But what we're doing "out there" is hard work. Everything that comes into a home, be it food, décor, clothing, or replacement parts, comes from somewhere. I remember one friend's comment, "My husband wants me to look like a million dollars, put meals on the table that are wonderful, and make this home look inviting, but he doesn't think I should take any time to shop for the contents to make that happen."

Christmas is a classic illustration of attending to incredible details that men would prefer dropping.

> Christmas shopping raises men's stress levels to those experienced by fighter pilots and riot police, according to psychologist David Lewis, who was recently asked to monitor heart rates, blood pressure and stress hormones among male shoppers at a London shopping center. He also found that, while men's stress levels sky-rocketed at the thought of buying presents, only one in four women even registered a slight change.[8]

## Investing Brings Dividends

Take what you've been given and make the most of it. You can also expect to reap only what you sow. "And let us not lose heart in doing good, for in due time we shall reap if we do not grow weary" (Gal. 6:9). "Present yourselves to God as those alive from the dead, and your members as instruments of righteousness to God," (Rom. 6:13). Attention to detail is a gift of God to women that makes us feel alive.

You can have a tremendous influence on the atmosphere of your world. Whether it's the color of paint, tone and volume of your voice, fragrance of the room, table settings, firmness of your mattress, food in your pantry[9] or other kinds of details, your care in investing "detailed expressions" multiplies God's intentions. And paying attention to God's interests brings dividends. This honors the Lord.

# Looking for Details that Need Not Be Lost

Luci Swindoll helps us feel the essence of beauty.

> It is born out of the commonplace, household life, personal relations, beating hearts, meeting eyes, poverty, necessity, hope, and fear. And finally, the real celebrating of its presence comes as we recall it in our memory, replaying the old records of our thoughts, gazing at the gallery of pictures with the eye of remembrance, and singing the song that is going on within us, a song to which we listen.[10]

In being a designer meant to beautify, we must look for the essence of beauty. We can multiply the effects we have on others through enjoying our wonderful female body, through transforming fragments into beauty, and through paying attention to details. Luci says this means "endeavoring to see that which is better than we know—it is capturing the splendor and spirit of the whole."[11] May you enjoy our God-given facets, and let them work for you, to be all you can be in reflecting the light from above.

# Conclusion

$\mathcal{F}$emininity! What is it? It's who I am as a woman. A calling. A challenge. An opportunity. A gift. It's a created design for fulfillment by God Himself. It's a matter of gender, being equal but different—in form and function.

We live in a society that shuns identification with gender. It's not particularly popular to be either a woman or a man. Every realm seeks to reduce the sexes to sameness, to a unisex pattern with uniform expectations and rules. Many push for equal provision with equal opportunity so nobody is different. Commonness is expected in coed dorms, coed army facilities, and in dress and physical requirements everywhere. Even a friend's computer rang alarm messages when entering a specific request for a gender definition. The computer's error message said, "Too gender specific." Even the computer bristled at gender issues.

# The Purpose of Femininity

Our purpose is to glorify God and to enjoy Him forever. To be truly image-bearers is to take what we've been given and maximize its effectiveness. The first step in being our best is to realize the value of the gem that we are. We are created to be an equal image-bearer with the man. We "are indeed fully equal to men in personhood, in importance and in status before God," as John Piper and Wayne Grudem say in *Recovering Biblical Manhood and Womanhood*.[1] We are equal, yet simultaneously we are very different—in body and in function. As we embrace, explore, and enhance these truths, we will have a glimpse of paradise. We will enjoy living out the truth and, thus, reflecting the light of God to a world that is grasping for His reality.

Regardless of a poor heritage, we can do as Philippians 3:13–14 advises, "Forgetting what lies behind and reaching forward to what lies ahead, I press on toward the goal for the prize of the upward call of God in Christ Jesus." If you have had poor role models and unfortunate circumstances with which to live, you can turn all the contorted confusion and turmoil over to the God of all wisdom and watch Him infuse your being with a sense of purpose.

As a feminine creation of Almighty God, you are marked for greatness. You are adequate. Capable. Gifted. Resourceful. Your femininity is His gift to you. Your uniqueness is like color—it creates different moods and adds vitality. Because you are different from man, you have unique facets through which you are privileged to reflect God's image.

# A Reflector of Light

Like a jewel, you are different from the next woman. But within your femininity, you possess similar facets out of which to reflect light, according to your own particular calling and gifting. *Woman of Splendor* has given us a picture of how God would have us maximize our strengths. Through the windows of the four facets of femininity can flow incredible displays of light.

*The Helpmate* mirrors the image of God through support, encouragement, and submission as modeled by the Son to the Father in heaven. A married woman supports her husband. A single woman can reflect these desired qualities within subordinate relationships at work, in the community, or at church.

*The Nurturer* has incredible opportunities to foster and empower relationships in many realms. Woman is a naturally gifted nurturer. The obvious sphere of effort is the development of future generations—the children in homes and neighborhoods everywhere.

*The Relater* links people and their needs with solutions that work. She also comforts others with her constant touch. Acting as a hub for critical development, her presence as a relational genius is only beginning to be appreciated.

*The Designer* enhances the world around her. As a woman gains awareness of her ability to bring pleasure to her family and her surroundings, she acquires added respect for herself. She transforms fragments into beauty by being so delightfully detail oriented. Bless her.

Jesus said, "I am the light of the world" (John 8:12). What a privilege we have to reflect His light through the facets He created in us. The purpose of our glorious femininity is wrapped up in Matthew 5:16: "'Let your light shine before men in such a way that they may see your good works, and glorify your Father who is in heaven.'"

❧

# *Appendix A* *Feeling Nurtured or Not*

## RESEARCH FOR WHY MOM IS IRREPLACEABLE IN THE FAMILY

"The young child's hunger for his mother's love and presence is as great as his hunger for food. And in consequence her absence inevitably generates a powerful sense of loss and anger." John Bowlby, *Attachment*, vol. 1 of *Attachment and Loss*, 2nd ed. (New York: Basic Books, 1982), xiii.

"When separation imperils that early attachment, it is difficult to build confidence, to build trust, to acquire the conviction that throughout the course of life we will—and deserve to—find others to meet our needs. And when our first connections are unreliable or broken or impaired, we may transfer that experience, and our responses to that experience, onto what we expect from our children, our friends, our marriage partner." Judith Viorst, *Necessary Losses* (New York: Simon and Schuster, 1986), 31.

*Developmental Psychology* reported studies conducted by Schwarz, Strickland, and Krolick that conclude that children "in day care from infancy . . . compared on nine behavioral traits with matched subjects who had no day care experience prior to the study were found to be significantly more aggressive, motorically active (more inclined to run about), and less cooperative with adults. . . . The infant group (day care from infancy) was also rated as more physically and verbally aggressive with peers and adults. There was a tendency for the infant group to be less tolerant of frustration. . . . The present findings suggest caution as we proceed into the day-care era." "Infant Day Care: Behavioral Effects at Preschool Age," *Developmental Psychology* 10 (1974): 502–506.

"There is an irreplaceable quality of a full-time mother. . . . One can't expect it to be done as well by other people. I am seeing more behavior disorders, early school problems, unconnected children, and children less focused, which I believe is directly related to mothers who are working full-time." Dr. Elmer Grossman, Berkley pediatric psychologist of twenty-seven years, quoted by Mary Farrar, "To Work or Not to Work: Making the Decision," reprinted by permission from the Marriage Life Conference, Family Life Ministry, 1988.

Psychologist Jay Belsky of Pennsylvania State University coauthored a report in 1978 concluding that day-care centers can be perfectly fine for young children. Eight years later (September 1986) Belsky reversed his earlier position in a report published in the journal *Zero to Three*. He concluded that babies who spend more than twenty hours a week in nonmaternal care during the first year of life risk having an "insecure attachment" to their mothers. Such children are more likely to become uncooperative and aggressive in early school years. His follow-up report in 1987 contended that even high-quality, stable, infant day care makes little difference.

A study by psychiatrist Peter Barglow of Chicago's Michael Reese Hospital concludes that even upper-middle-class one-year-olds, enjoying ostensibly the best substitute care (at home with a nanny or baby-sitter) tend to be less securely attached to their mothers. "Is the mother by far the best caretaker for the child in the first year?" asks Barglow. "We think probably yes." *Time*, 22 June 1987.

"In the years when baby and his parents make their first enduring human partnerships, when love, trust, joy, and self-evaluation emerge . . . millions of small children in our land may be learning values for survival in our baby banks. They may learn the rude justice of the communal playpen . . . or they may learn that all adults are interchangeable, that love is capricious, that human attachment is a perilous investment. . . . Children reared without an enduring relationship with a mother figure seem incapable of sustaining lasting relationships later in life." Selma Fraiberg, *Every Child's Birthright: In Defense of Mothering*, (New York: Basic Books, 1977).

Dr. David Elkind, author of several books and chairman of the Department of Child Study at Tufts University, Medford, Massachusetts, is so deeply concerned about this issue that he has written a book on the subject. He has noted an increased number of children in his practice who are showing the same signs of stress that have long been identified in adults. One of the reasons for this, he notes, is the increase in both parents working. "Working parents, particularly mothers, are of necessity more stressed . . . than are non-working parents." Dr.

Elkind goes on to say that children are expected to adapt to their parents' schedules and stressed lifestyles, and their parents tend to push them to grow up quickly . . . all of which children are not equipped to handle. David Elkind, *The Hurried Child* (Reading, Mass.: Addison-Wesley, 1981), 39.

Referring to the day-care center, Noma Hardwick says, "I am concerned about our present day care situation. The ratio of worker to child is too low, thus providing minimal care and attention to the individual child and his needs. Day care workers receive minimum wages, resulting in a rapid turnover of workers and lack of consistency for the child. The requirements and educational expectations of the worker are very low. Children who come from the day care rigor into first grade tend to be less secure, more clingy, less focused and disciplined. They seem to need much more love and touching. We are in for a rude awakening if something is not done." Noma Hardwick, 1985 California Nursery School Teacher of the Year. Quoted by Farrar, Marriage Life Conference, 1988.

"Children can thrive on good-sized portions of rice and beans and corn; they would soon starve on one bite a day of filet mignon. . . . Because parents are so activity-oriented, they tend to rate time spent 'doing things' with their children as constructive and ignore the rest. . . . What that mother does not realize is that to a young child, her presence, even in another room, makes a big difference. . . . To her child, the ability to touch base makes all the difference in the world." William and Wendy Dreskin, "The Case Against Day Care," *San Francisco Chronicle*. The Dreskins write out of their own experience of running a nonprofit day-care center for the benefit of their community and in an effort to help meet the needs of children requiring day care. After deciding that what they were seeing even at their own day-care center was not beneficial to children, they eventually closed their center and wrote a book based on their research and experience.

"We are much more likely to have our quality moments when we are around our kids more. Quantity time is 'real life'—going to the grocery store, hanging around the kitchen together, driving around in the car pools. It's all the different responses in a million circumstances every day." Deborah Fallows, *A Mother's Work* (Boston: Houghton Mifflin, 1985).

"Quality time for a four-year-old may be having Mommie there to kiss a scrape and apply a bandage. A nine-year-old may consider it quality time if Mom is available to talk as soon as he bursts through the front door after school. . . . Quality time for our children often defies advance scheduling. We may fool ourselves to think that quality time is time scheduled for our convenience. But we won't fool our children." Jean Fleming, *A Mother's Heart* (Colorado Springs, Colo: NavPress, 1982).

(Thanks to Brenda Hunter and Mary Farrar for pointing me to this research.)

# Appendix B
# Being a Hub
# in the Home

## "THINGS DON'T JUST HAPPEN"

- Arrange dinner for friends/business associates
- Frame and/or hang pictures
- Forward the letters
- Pick up stamps
- Drop off and pick up the dry cleaning
- Wash laundry
- Prepare meals and snacks
- "Could we put that away?"
- "Can you call _____ back for me?"
- "Did you turn in the film?"
- Explain needs to the repairman
- Mail that item
- "Could you wrap up _____ to send?"
- Find the escaped dog or cat
- Pass on the phone messages via E-mail
- "Could you help me with _____?"

- Buy a gift for _____
- Order that _____
- Help the neighbors with their animals
- Suggest entertainment ideas
- Send a card to _____
- Remind others to talk to _____
- Arrange the airplane tickets
- "Do we have a car rented?"
- Manage the laundry
- Find missing underwear and socks
- Make sure those hoses are moved
- Get bids on the deck
- Call an exterminator, and let him in
- Renew magazines
- Locate an electrician
- Balance checkbooks
- Keep home clean, organized, and smelling good
- Don't miss that meeting
- Order more checks
- Gather the mail; respond to it
- Invite and entertain guests
- Return the library books
- Call in, pick up prescriptions
- Return RSVPs
- Entertain out-of-town guests
- Get freezer checked and defrosted
- Check E-mail; answer messages
- Look for new furniture item
- Keep lawn looking nice
- Organize décor
- Place order for house or clothing item
- Rearrange phone service
- Schedule oil change in that car, maintenance too
- Change that bed for guests
- Fill cars with gas
- Buy/make a dessert for _____
- "Can you make sure we received a credit?"
- "Can I have the barbeque here?"
- "Did you record _____ for me?"
- "Would you scratch my back?"
- "Would you rub my legs?"

- "Are you ready to leave yet?"
- "We need to drop by _____."
- "We need to attend _____."
- "We should help _____."
- Remind others to clear clutter
- Grocery shop
- "Did you connect with _____?"
- "Could you research the price for _____?"
- "What did _____ say about _____?"
- "File this please"
- "I need a _____ "
- "Could you exchange _____?"
- Plant flowers and weed flowerbeds
- Send a check to _____
- Take pet to the vet
- Find the newspaper
- Attend meetings with financial/legal associates
- Plan family gatherings
- Wrap and mail the gifts
- Get rackets strung
- Call the plumber and work on the toilet
- Keep the shelves stocked—food, cleaning supplies, paper supplies, batteries, light bulbs, shoe polish
- Talk to accountant
- Verify airline mileage to be credited
- Make copies of _____
- Update activity calendar
- Make and take a meal for _____
- Do the mending
- Send the thank-yous
- Get tree evaluated and fertilized
- Organize receipted items
- Get maps for _____
- Retrace steps on bank statement
- Make bank deposits
- Make and keep up with medical appointments
- Keep a ledger of expenses

(You can add much to this list.)

❧

# *Appendix C*
# *Being a Hub*
# *with Children*

FOUNDATIONALLY, YOU WILL:
- Relay the pleasure of your acceptance of them and their importance
- Draw them near to all that is important
- Remind them of your support and love
- Oversee continual choices
- Hear the heartaches to steer hearts toward healing
- Refresh concerned spirits
- Help ease the pain along the way
- Reinforce good decisions
- Model God's principles for them to follow
- Present scenarios before trouble erupts
- Create good feelings during all seasons
- Anticipate their every need
- Look for opportunities to help them shine, and take action
- Make positive connections with your eyes, heart, and spirit
- Tie together loose ends they can't visualize

- Build the foundational issues first
- Guide them into better choices
- Ease anxious feelings
- "Feel out" the situation at hand
- Help them find higher ground during difficulty
- Provide ongoing encouragement
- Demonstrate ways to make things happen
- Teach life skills continually
- Provide security with even your presence
- Show interest in their world
- Referee battles
- Look out for trouble spots
- Calm their fears
- Praise the diligent
- Give hands-on assistance
- Smooth the way
- Watch for danger/disasters (foresee) and protect
- Find the safe way for them
- Place careful boundaries
- Stop destructive choices
- Lead them into positive patterns
- Enact the smartest plan
- Offer "I'm here for you" attitude
- Provide wisdom/direction
- Keep taking them back to God "through it all"
- Expend your energy with purpose
- Pursue positive progress always
- Intercede in prayer for moment-by-moment needs
- Give of yourself, whether it's deserved or not
- Approach maturely all concerns
- Communicate at a soul level
- Maintain the organization of scheduling
- Find missing pieces for everybody's "puzzle"

PRACTICALLY, YOU WILL:
- Talk to, interact with, pursue
- Feed, bathe, change clothes
- Rock, read to, watch, play with
- Take to church, school, relatives', library, friends' houses, sports events, practices, games, recitals, music lessons, doctor, dentist, orthodontist

- Attend their developed interest presentations
- Listen to
- Pray with and for
- Praise them, compliment them
- Help with projects
- Ask about feelings
- Eat with
- Vacation with
- Have fun with
- Give advice
- Share the rules
- Discipline
- Show pleasure over them
- Smile at
- Encourage their giftedness and interests
- Show interest
- Spend time with
- Play games with
- Make their favorite foods
- Honor their birthdays and special days
- Attend their honor events
- Sacrifice for their needs
- Hold them physically
- Encourage friendships
- Make eye contact
- Make provision for things to happen
- Arrange for baby-sitters

(You can add much to this list.)

NOTE: The interest shown and energy spent sends messages of importance, value, worth, acceptance, care, sacrifice, security, stability, interest, purpose, heart, and honor. Are we willing to forgo any of these messages because we are too busy, too tired, too stressed, too divided, too selfish, or too whatever?

# Appendix D
# Being a Hub in an Office/Business/Life Setting

- Possess winsome feminine charm that attracts positive connections
- Activate antenna skills to keep in touch with everything
- Know who to call and keep connecting with them
- Remember adequate supplies
- Acquire knowledge of how to _____
- Use discretion with tough personalities
- Sense how to deal best with hard issues
- Look for details to take care of
- Honor others' interests
- Pick up on innuendoes
- Put people together who will help the cause
- Look for the best options

- Coordinate the scheduling
- Pursue the most excellent way for the group
- Be sensitive to saving money
- Be skillful at managing funds
- Be aware of many factors to be considered
- Be diligent to pursue the task at hand
- Use gracious tactics to motivate
- Desire to get the job done well
- Gather lots of information to work with
- Draw many together on the united effort
- Keep working until the tasks are complete
- Foster the abilities of others
- Remember and incorporate all the details
- Find new ways to cover more details
- Draw together the strengths of others
- Watch for little dangers that could stop the whole project
- Inform the right people to help avoid disasters
- Sense how to pull it all together
- Motivate others skillfully to meet the needs at hand
- Diligently pursue details—don't wait for someone to "baby-sit" you
- Communicate continually to avoid confusion, misunderstanding, or a loss of contract
- Communicate continually to motivate, encourage, reassure future contacts, and reinforce positive behavior

(You can add much to this list.)

# Study Questions

## Chapter 1—Confusing Images

1. What are some words or phrases that are used when women describe their inner struggles regarding femininity?
2. What are some negative cultural trends that could affect your life too easily?
3. What are some Scriptures to rehearse which will cause our minds to rest in the Creator's design for each of us?
4. What specific confusion about being a woman do you desire to more clearly understand?
5. Are you feeling "sacrifice" or "privilege" as you live the life of a woman, and why?

## Chapter 2—Biblical Authority

1. Why is it so important that we decide what authority we choose to follow in life? How does this choice relate to what we think about our femininity?

2. What makes God's design right, over our personal preference?

3. What are some Scriptures which remind us to pursue a godly base, rather than our natural bent?

4. Describe the foundation on which you are building your plan for life. Is it strong enough to enable your facing hard issues without destruction?

5. Could we fool ourselves into thinking that we are in God's will, and yet not accept His declared designs for life?

## Chapter 3—Differences Between Masculine and Feminine

1. Name ten differences between masculine and feminine that affect you most every day.

2. How does rehearsing the differences between men and women help you understand yourself and your response?

3. How does rehearsing the differences between men and women help you in relating to men in general? (Consult my husband Stu's chart on what the four pillars of a man's heart are like—page 33.)

4. What does the devil want to destroy and promote when attacking us regarding our gender differences?

5. How can your renewed awareness of differences honor God now or in future generations?

## Chapter 4—The Jewel of Femininity

1. After studying the chart/diagram of the Jewel of Femininity (page 34), suggest practical ways a woman can live out the positive descriptions of reflecting light through each facet.
   • Partnering to support, to encourage
   • Developing to foster, to empower
   • Connecting to link, to comfort
   • Beautifying to adorn, to enhance

2. Also after studying this same chart/diagram, suggest real-life negative possibilities that a woman needs to strive to avoid where she might withhold reflecting light through each facet.
   • A helpmate who: destroys dominates, diminishes
   • A nurturer who: demolishes, deprives, discourages
   • A relater who: distracts, disengages, distances
   • A designer who: darkens, degrades, dismantles

## Chapter 5—A Helpmate Suitable

1. What are some key elements in developing our attitude toward being the kind of helpmate God would desire?
2. What Scriptures tell us this facet is more than God's casual idea?
3. What profile qualities does He expect us to possess and to demonstrate?
4. As a helpmate, what will your life look like if you are "accessible" and "giving of yourself"?
5. Will a helpmate always "feel" like being a superwoman? What factors should she remember at all times?

## Chapter 6—Commitment, Submission, and Rebellion

1. What requirements are made of us when we make a marriage commitment? Refer to Scripture.
2. Rehearse the model of submission we have in Eph. 5:25–27 and 1 Peter 2:21–24.
3. Study the chart on page 82 and determine at least five new ways you can activate your love to Christ through your response to Christ's example of biblical submission, as to your husband.
4. Become familiar with misconceptions about submission and discuss how you can avoid wrong choices.
5. Discuss rebellion to submission—then consider how and why submission is a positive concept for us to fulfill in our daily lives.

## Chapter 7—Building Your Marriage

1. Make a list of the ten ways you can support and encourage your husband.
2. Which two suggestions sparked your attention most to motivate new approaches in building your man?
3. Share some victories you've experienced that could lend a positive power of suggestion to your peers.
4. Make a list of how you could be increasingly positive in building your man.
5. In passing on a strong marital legacy, what are some definite factors you will seek to model to your children?

## Chapter 8—The Nurturing Process

1. Compare what you do with the black and white lines of a coloring book to how you develop a child after the act of birth.

2. Compare the farmer's work with the nurturing mother's work as shown at a glance on the tree chart, page 103. Discuss how you observe a lengthy process needed to indeed develop a product.

3. Read Proverbs 22:6 after studying the tree chart. Describe thoughts you have as you further develop the meaning of those words, *train up*, and how extensive that process can be.

4. Look at the iceberg diagram on page 106. Since so much of our nurturing process is not easily seen (below the surface of physical provisions), what are some specifics of emotional and spiritual provision we must offer in helping our children be whole?

5. Verbalize any new commitment you are making in regard to your supporting, protecting, and being available to meet needs of your kids.

6. Comment on the "messages" needing to be sent in life as reflected on the "Impact" chart, page 118.

## Chapter 9—Feeling Nurtured or Not

1. Share some positive feelings you may have identified to be noticeable in your children's lives. (See chart on page 124 for ideas.)

2. Identify any negative feelings you may be observing in your child and zero in on the reasons behind them. (Ask a prayer partner to pray for the necessary changes.)

3. Look through the list of positive actions you have been living out, as shown on the "Nurtured or Not" chart (page 124) and share some success stories you have experienced.

4. Privately evaluate any negative profile you possess (on right side of the chart, page 124) so the appropriate feelings being developed can change. (Again, ask a prayer partner to pray for any needed changes.)

5. Discuss any especially relevant revelations you may have become more acutely aware of regarding the correlation of mom's nurturing and the feelings a child develops appropriately.

6. List a few facts from the research in Appendix A, page 220) that if closely adhered to could encourage a more stable society in which children felt nurtured.

## Chapter 10—Letting Go—the Culmination

1. List some of those many stages of letting go of children, starting with the cutting of the umbilical cord. List other types of letting go also, regarding nurturing opportunities.
2. Go down the list, and describe what it would be like, NOT to cut that physical umbilical cord, NOT quit feeding that child yourself, etc.
3. Read Genesis 2:24, Matthew 19:4–6, and Ephesians 5:31. Identify the clear message portrayed and write a few sentences with your name in them as to how it applies to you.
4. What is the correlation between selfishness and letting go?
5. How would a truly released "child/adult" and his or her spouse describe this healthy position. (Take clues from the chapter, the "Apron Strings" poem at the beginning, and/or from healthy examples around you.)

## Chapter 11—The Relational Genius

1. Rehearse some facts given that help you understand a woman's reputation to be a relational genius.
2. Discuss the parallels of God to woman, with connection abilities and power. See John 3:5, 6, 8; John 14:16–17; John 14:18.
3. Suggest some major differences we generally observe between man and woman when it comes to connecting with relationships.
4. Is there a "down side" to woman's relational abilities?
5. Read Proverbs 31:26. Name five examples of how you can fulfill this today.

## Chapter 12—Importance of Being a Hub

1. Describe some of the benefits those around you experience when you truly function as a hub.
2. What are some suggested pictures of being a hub which you can transfer to your world of activity, visualizing how your connection power makes or breaks your world?
3. Look over the "hub connections" lists in the home, with children or in the office/life setting in Appendices B, C, and D and mark all the ways you make a difference as a hub. What would you add to the list?
4. Discuss how the small things a hub does can create big results.

5. Think about society's children-at-large being able to experience the love of a hub in a home. Because of all the connection of loose ends below the surface, describe some confident feelings of self-worth that can result from this worthy profession.

## Chapter 13—Connecting Past to Present and Future

1. Name some practical ways suggested in the chapter to accomplish this mission of connecting the past to the present and the future.
2. Think of other ways you have made these connections.
3. Read Psalm 102:18–22, Romans 15:4, and Deuteronomy 5:29. If God uses past events to bring profit and meaning to future generations, are we seeing the value to follow His pattern in the setting He has placed us? Share the profits you see as we learn the art of connecting.
4. What could happen in your life to help make connecting easier? Is there some relational healing that you want to work on?
5. Whether you've been creative in the past or not, can you think of one way you could make some sort of new connection of the past to the present or to the future? (Make today the new start.)

## Chapter 14—The Wonderful Feminine Body

1. What would you communicate to someone who was inquiring about why the feminine body should be discussed in this book?
2. Rehearse some Scriptures that refer to the body being important.
3. Why should we enhance our bodies?
4. What can we do ourselves and how might we encourage the next generation in making the most of our appearance?
5. Discuss the element of balance, so as to avoid becoming over- or under-focused on the body's importance.

## Chapter 15—Transforming Fragments into Beauty

1. When you think of a woman "nesting," what do you see her doing?
2. How does Jesus go before us and provide a pattern to follow?
3. What and how have you made specific things beautiful out of very little to work with?
4. Because we learn by watching others, share how you've learned to create various touches of beauty.

5. Do you feel good about leaving things in fragments, or creating order out of voids? Do you feel a sort of rest for your soul with beauty? Elaborate.

## Chapter 16—Expression Made through Details

1. Think of a true story from your life where details were extremely important to your world. Describe it.
2. How does it feel when you weave a myriad of details to develop a beautiful product? Explain.
3. How does God go before us in paying attention to details? Discuss how He created our brains.
4. Can a woman feel good about being detail-oriented when her husband might not understand? Why? Discuss this.
5. Finish this sentence, "Details express _____."

## Conclusion

1. Reflect on any renewed appreciation you have for being a woman.
2. What thought(s) has (have) revived your hope for being who you really are inside?
3. Is there something that you can run harder with because it has come into focus?
4. How can you encourage other women (including your own daughters and/or granddaughters) to maximize their self-esteem as a woman?
5. Are you committing forever to play in your mind the positive messages of God's incredible design for your womanhood?

# *Endnotes*

## Chapter 1

1. F. Carolyn Graglia, *Domestic Tranquility* (Dallas, Tex.: Spence, 1998), 24–25.
2. John Piper and Wayne Grudem, *Recovering Biblical Manhood and Womanhood* (Wheaton, Ill.: Crossway, 1991), xxvi.
3. Elisabeth Elliot, "Virginity," *Elisabeth Elliot Newsletter*, March/April 1990 (Ann Arbor, Mich.: Servant), 3.
4. Linda Weber, *Mom, You're Incredible* (Nashville, Tenn.: Broadman & Holman, 1999), 73–80.

## Chapter 2

1. Ruth Myers, *31 Days of Praise* (Sisters, Ore.: Multnomah, 1994), 55.
2. Joshua 24:15.

## Chapter 3

1. Stu Weber, *Tender Warrior* (Sisters, Ore.: Multnomah, 1993), 121–22.
2. Thomas Boslooper and Marcia Hayes, *The Femininity Game* (New York: Sein and Day, 1973), 148.

3. Stu Weber, *Four Pillars of a Man's Heart* (Sisters, Ore. : Multnomah, 1997), 63.

4. John Piper and Wayne Grudem, *Recovering Biblical Manhood and Womanhood* (Wheaton, Ill.: Crossway, 1991).

5. As quoted in the *FamilyLife Marriage Conference Manual*, p. 111, Paul Popenoe, "Are Women Really Different?" February 1991.

6. As quoted in the *FamilyLife Marriage Conference Manual*, p. 112, Jo Durden-Smith and Diane DeSimone, "Is There a Superior Sex?" *Readers Digest*, November 1982.

7. Christine Gorman, "Sizing up the Sexes," *Time*, 20 January 1992, 42.

8. As listed in the *FamilyLife Marriage Conference Manual*, 1995, 85.

9. Gary Smalley with Steve Scott, *For Better or for Best* (Grand Rapids, Mich.: Zondervan, 1982), 29.

10. Dee Brestin, "Speaking Different Languages," *Moody Monthly*, July/August 1992, 18–20.

11. Willard F. Harley Jr., *His Needs, Her Needs* (Old Tappan, N.J.: Fleming H. Revell, 1986), 176–77.

12. Susan Hunt, *True Woman* (Wheaton, Ill.: Crossway, 1997), 221.

13. Deborah Newman, *Then God Created Woman* (Colorado Springs, Colo.: Focus on the Family, 1997), 218.

14. Joan Shapiro, with George Hartlaub, *Men: A Translation for Women* (New York: Dutton, 1991), 235.

## Chapter 4

1. Ingrid Trobisch with Marlee Alex, *Keeper of the Springs* (Sisters, Ore.: Multnomah, 1997), 64.

2. Carol Brazo, *No Ordinary Home* (Sisters, Ore.: Multnomah, 1995), 48.

3. Trobisch with Alex, *Keeper of the Springs*, 71.

4. Ibid., 26.

## Chapter 5

1. Toni Grant, *Being a Woman—Fulfilling Your Femininity and Finding Love* (New York: Random House, 1988), preface ix, x.

2. Ibid., 177.

3. Joyce Landorf Heatherley, *Balcony People* (Austin, Tex.: Balcony, 1984), 12.

4. Ibid., 15–16.

5. Ibid., 69.

6. Jo Stone, *Give Him His Gate* (Houston, Tex.: Spring Branch Community Church, 1975), 6–7.

7. Mart DeHaan, "Times of Discovery," *News and Comments:* 60, no. 3, March-April, 1.

8. Alice Gray, Mom-to-Mom Lecture (Good Shepherd Community Church, Boring, Ore., February 1998).

9. Andy Stanley, "Prevailing Love" (series delivered to his church in Alpharetta, Ga., North Point Community Church, January-March, 1998), tape 98B01.

## Chapter 6

1. Deborah Newman, *Then God Created Woman* (Colorado Springs, Colo.: Focus on the Family Publishing, 1997), 230.
2. Ruth Myers, *31 Days of Praise* (Sisters, Ore.: Multnomah, 1994), 120–21.
3. Ibid., 121.
4. Ruth Senter, *Have We Really Come a Long Way? Regaining What Feminism Has Stolen from Christian Women* (Minneapolis, Minn.: Bethany House, 1997), 138.
5. Jo Stone, *Give Him His Gate* (Houston, Tex.: Spring Branch Community Church, 1975), 24.
6. Joyce Landorf Heatherley, *Balcony People* (Austin, Tex.: Balcony, 1984), 57.
7. Deanna McClary with Jerry B. Jenkins, *Commitment to Love* (Pawleys Island, S.C.: Clebe McClary, Inc., 1989), 126–28.
8. Susan Hunt, *The True Woman* (Wheaton, Ill.: Crossway, 1997), 218.
9. Robert Lewis and William Hendricks, *Rocking the Roles* (Colorado Springs, Colo.: Navpress, 1991), 136.
10. Hunt, *The True Woman*, 223.
11. Joy P. Gage, *But You Don't Know Harry* (Wheaton, Ill.: Tyndale House, 1972).
12. Christine McClelland, "That Ugly 'S' Word," *Moody Monthly*, July/August 1998, 48.
13. Christine McClelland, "God's Opinion about Wifely Submission," *Current Thoughts and Trends*, November 1998, 9.

## Chapter 7

1. Stu Weber, *Tender Warrior* (Sisters, Ore.: Multnomah, 1993), 35ff.
2. Stu Weber, *All the Kings Men* (Sister, Ore.: Multnomah, 1998), 155–56.
3. Mike Yorkey, *Saving Money Any Way You Can* (Ann Arbor, Mich.: Servant, 1994).
4. John Piper, *What's the Difference?* (Westchester, Ill.: Crossway, 1990), 37.
5. Richard L. Strauss, *How to Raise Confident Children* (Grand Rapids, Mich.: Baker, 1975), 120, 131.
6. James Dobson, *Love Must Be Tough* (Dallas, Tex.: Word, 1983).
7. Dennis Rainey, *My Soapbox* (newsletter for Family Ministry), 10 October 1988, 1.
8. Lois Mowday Rabey, *The Snare* (Colorado Springs, Colo.: NavPress, 1988).

## Chapter 8

1. Matthew Fordahl, "Family Mourns Murdered Child," (Portland) *Oregonian*, 20 October 1994.
2. Mortimer B. Zuckerman, "Attention Must Be Paid," *US News and World Report*, 25 August 1997, 92.
3. Ingrid Trobisch with Marlee Alex, *Keeper of the Springs* (Sisters, Ore.: Multnomah, 1997), 47.
4. Gary Bauer, "What Aren't We Teaching Our Children?" *Focus on the Family Citizen*, 12 May 1998, no. 5: 22.

5. Sandy Lynam Clough, *Heirlooms from Loving Hands*, (Eugene, Ore.: Harvest House, 1998), 44.
6. Karen Moderow, "Choosing Home," *Moody Monthly*, February 1994, 14, 16.
7. Ken Magid and Carole A. McKelvey, *High Risk* (Lakewood, Colo.: CDR Distributors, Bantam, 1987), 62.
8. Linda Burton, Janet Dittmer, Cheri Loveless, *What's a Smart Woman like You Doing at Home?* (Vienna, Va.: Mothers at Home, 1992), 42.

## Chapter 9

1. Anne Morrow Lindbergh, *Gift from the Sea* (New York: Random House, 1978), 46–47.
2. Edith Schaeffer, *What Is a Family?* (Old Tappan, N.J.: Fleming H. Revell, 1975), 94.
3. Ingrid Trobisch with Marlee Alex, *Keeper of the Springs* (Sisters, Ore.: Multnomah, 1997), 38.
4. Stephen R. Covey, "Religious Faith Vital in Today's 'Nation in Crisis'," *USA Today*, 2 October 1997, 7D.
5. Jean Lush, *Mothers and Sons* (Grand Rapids, Mich.: Fleming H. Revell, 1988), 104.
6. Joan Shapiro, M.D., *Men—A Translation for Women*, (New York: Dutton, 1992), 65.
7. Ibid., 44.
8. Lush, *Mothers and Sons*, 106.
9. Gary Fields, "1.6 Million Kids Home Alone," *USA TODAY*, May 1994.
10. Bettijane Levine, "Dr. Spock, 91, Tries Again," (Portland) *Oregonian*, 3 September 1994, C4.
11. Suzanne Fields, "Feminism's Path from Seneca Falls," *Insight*, 24 August 1998, 48.
12. Lush, *Mothers and Sons*, 103.
13. Peter and Barbara Wyden, *Growing Up Straight* (New York: New American Library, 1968), 41.
14. Lush, *Mothers and Sons*, 106.
15. Ken Hoffman, "Community Failed Teen Crying Out for Help," *USA Today*, 26 May 1998.
16. Ashbel S. Green, Janet Filips, Dana Tims, and Brian T. Meehan, "The Suspect: Kipland Kinkel's Dark Side Was No Secret to His Peers," *Oregonian*, 22 May 1998, A1, 21, 23.
17. Joe Hallinan, "Fear of Young People Grows—with Reason," *Oregonian*, 5 May 1994, A4.
18. Romel Hernandez, "Young Blood," *Oregonian*, 11 February 1996, G4.
19. Brenda Hunter, *The Power of Mother Love* (Colorado Springs, Colo.: WaterBrook, 1997), 235.
20. Linda Weber, *Mom, You're Incredible* (Nashville, Tenn.: Broadman & Holman, 1999).

## Chapter 10

1. Carol Kuykendall, "Celebrating the Empty Nest," *Virtue*, October/November 1998, 44.

2. Henry Cloud and John Townsend, *The Mom Factor* (Grand Rapids, Mich.: Zondervan, 1996), 196–97.

3. Ibid., 196.

4. Ibid., 220.

5. Ruth Myers, *31 Days of Praise* (Sisters, Ore.: Multnomah, 1994), 77.

6. Carol Kuykendall, *Learning To Let Go* (Grand Rapids, Mich.: Zondervan, 1985), 9.

7. Ibid., 37.

8. Cloud and Townsend, *The Mom Factor*, 96.

9. Ibid., 97.

10. Carol Kuykendall, *Learning To Let Go*, 11.

11. Erma Bombeck, *Motherhood: The Second Oldest Profession* (New York: N.Y.: Dell, 1983), 30.

12. Ingrid Trobisch with Marlee Alex, *Keeper of the Springs* (Sisters, Ore.: Multnomah, 1997), 56.

13. Cloud and Townsend, *The Mom Factor*, 99.

14. James Osterhaus, *Rewriting the Stories that Made You Who You Are* (Downers Grove, Ill.: InterVarsity, 1997), 1.

15. Trobisch with Alex, *Keeper of the Springs*, 75–76.

16. Ibid.

17. Ibid.

18. Cloud and Townsend, *The Mom Factor*, 205.

19. Erma Bombeck, as quoted in *Our Daily Bread*, 16 August 1994 (Grand Rapids, Mich.: RBC Ministries), by J. David Branon.

## Chapter 11

1. Anastasia Toufexis, "Coming from a Different Place," *Time* (special edition), Fall 1990, 65.

2. Jo Durden-Smith and Diane DeSimone, "Is There a Superior Sex?" *Readers Digest*, November 1982.

3. Christine Gorman, "Sizing Up the Sexes," *Time*, 20 January 1992, 42.

4. Ibid., 44.

5. Ibid.

6. Dee Brestin, "Why Women Need Other Women" *Moody*, July/August 1992, p. 26.

7. Henry Cloud and John Townsend, *The Mom Factor* (Grand Rapids, Mich.: Zondervan, 1996), 221.

8. Gorman, "Sizing Up the Sexes," 45.

9. Ingrid Trobisch with Marlee Alex, *Keeper of the Springs* (Sisters, Ore.: Multnomah, 1997), 67–68.

10. Ibid., 68.

11. Anastasia Toufexis, "Coming from a Different Place," 65.

12. Terry Willits, *Creating a SenseSational Home* (Grand Rapids, Mich.: Zondervan, 1996), 10, 22.

13. Proverbs 2:16–17; 6:24–25; 7:10–13, 16–18, 21; 9:13; 23:27–28; 30:20.
14. Proverbs 21:9, 19; 25:24; 27:15.
15. Proverbs 15:4; Colossians 4:6; Proverbs 10:11; 12:18; 21:23; 25:11; 10:19.

## Chapter 12

1. Chuck Swindoll, Wheaton College commencement address (Wheaton, Ill., May 1991).
2. Terry Willits, *Creating a SenseSational Home* (Grand Rapids, Mich.: Zondervan, 1996), 23.
3. Ingrid Trobisch with Marlee Alex, *Keeper of the Springs* (Sisters, Ore.: Multnomah Publishers, 1997), 79.
4. Joy Jacobs and Deborah Strubel, *Single, Whole, and Holy* (Camp Hill, Penn.: Horizon Books, 1996), 1973.
5. Barbara Bush, as quoted by James Dobson and Gary L. Bauer, *Children at Risk* (Dallas, Tex: Word, 1990), 157.

## Chapter 13

1. Interview with Barry Arnold at Good Shepherd Community Church, Boring, Ore., 2 November 1998.
2. Sandy Lynam Clough, *Heirlooms from Loving Hands* (Eugene, Ore.: Harvest House, 1998), 26.
3. Ingrid Trobisch with Marlee Alex, *Keeper of the Springs* (Sisters, Ore.: Multnomah, 1997), 13.
4. Mary Kay Shanley, *The Memory Box* (Marshalltown, Iowa: Sta-Kris, 1996), book jacket.
5. Ro Logrippo, "Picture This," (Portland) *Oregonian*, 12 May 1994, Living/Family Life section, CO1.
6. Shanley, *The Memory Box*, 46.

## Chapter 14

1. Judith Couchman, *The Woman Behind the Mirror* (Nashville, Tenn.: Broadman & Holman, 1997), 4.
2. Cynthia Hicks and Karen Lee-Thorp, *Why Beauty Matters* (Colorado Springs, Colo.: NavPress, 1977), 148–49.

## Chapter 15

1. Stu Weber, *Tender Warrior* (Sisters, Ore.: Multnomah, 1993), 106.
2. Terry Willits, *Creating a SenseSational Home* (Grand Rapids, Mich.: Zondervan, 1996), 15.
3. Susan Hunt, *The True Woman* (Wheaton, Ill.: Crossway, 1997), 187.
4. Tracy Porter, *Returning Home* (Kansas City, Kan.: Andrews & McMeel, 1997), 1–2.

5. Willits, *Creating a SenseSational Home*, 9.
6. Porter, *Returning Home*, 23.
7. Ibid., 20.
8. Sandy Lynam Clough, *Heirlooms from Loving Hands* (Eugene, Ore.: Harvest House, 1998), 4.
9. Ecclesiastes 1:9.

## Chapter 16

1. Taken off the Internet, "Are Men and Women Really the Same?"
2. Christine Gorman, "Sizing Up the Sexes," *Time*, 20 January 1992, 46.
3. Ibid., 45.
4. Ibid.
5. Ibid.
6. Ibid.
7. Terry Willits, *Creating a SenseSational Home* (Grand Rapids, Mich.: Zondervan, 1996), 16.
8. "Different Drumbeats," *Focus on the Family*, "The Pastor's Weekly Briefing," Vol. 6, No. 49, 4 December 1998, 2.
9. Willits, 17.
10. Luci Swindoll, *You Bring the Confetti—God Brings the Joy* (Dallas, Tex.: Word, 1986), 142–43.
11. Ibid., 140.

## Conclusion

1. John Piper and Wayne Grudem, *Recovering Biblical Manhood and Womanhood* (Wheaton, Ill.: Crossway, 1991), xiv.

～

Linda can be contacted at the following address:

Linda Weber
2229 NE Burnside St., #212
Gresham, OR 97030